GRIT BLOCS

100 OF THE FINEST
BOULDER PROBLEMS
ON PENNINE GRITSTONE

GRIT BLOCS

DAVE PARRY

Vertebrate Publishing, Sheffield
www.adventurebooks.com

GRIT BLOCS

100 OF THE FINEST BOULDER PROBLEMS ON PENNINE GRITSTONE

DAVE PARRY

First published in 2022 by **Vertebrate Publishing**.

VERTEBRATE PUBLISHING
Omega Court, 352 Cemetery Road, Sheffield S11 8FT, United Kingdom.
www.adventurebooks.com

Copyright © 2022 Dave Parry and Vertebrate Publishing Ltd.
Foreword copyright © 2022 Dan Turner.

Front cover Gwyneth Uttley on *Brain Dead*, Cratcliffe Tor.
Back cover, top left Rob Smith on *Chabal*, Gorple. **Top right** Ned Feehally on *Brainstorm*, Doll Tor. **Bottom left** Frances Bensley on *Boyager*, Burbage North. **Bottom right** Rob Smith on *The Scientist*, Great Roova.

Pages xii–1 John Coefield on *Beth's Traverse*, Goldsborough Carr.
Pages 8–9 Lower Gorple.
Pages 96–97 *Elemental*, Thorn Crag.
Pages 106–107 Stanage Plantation area.

Photography by Dave Parry unless otherwise credited.

Dave Parry has asserted his rights under the Copyright, Designs and Patents Act 1988 to be identified as author of this work.

A CIP catalogue record for this book is available from the British Library.

ISBN 978-1-83981-162-3

All rights reserved. No part of this work covered by the copyright herein may be reproduced or used in any form or by any means – graphic, electronic, or mechanised, including photocopying, recording, taping, or information storage and retrieval systems – without the written permission of the publisher.

Edited by Helen Parry, map by Jane Beagley, **www.adventurebooks.com**

Production by Terry Yeardley, C2 Clear Creative. Based on an original design by Les Éditions du Mont-Blanc.

Printed and bound in Europe by Latitude Press.

Vertebrate Publishing is committed to printing on paper from sustainable sources.

Climbing is an activity that carries a risk of personal injury or death. Participants must be aware of and accept that these risks are present and they should be responsible for their own actions and involvement. Nobody involved in the writing and production of this book accepts any responsibility for any errors that it may contain, or are they liable for any injuries or damage that may arise from its use. All climbing is inherently dangerous and the fact that individual descriptions in this volume do not point out such dangers does not mean that they do not exist. Take care.

CONTENTS

FOREWORD vi

INTRODUCTION viii

GRITSTONE – BEHIND THE SCENES x

100 OF THE FINEST BOULDER PROBLEMS
North Pennines xii
Yorkshire 8
Lancashire 96
Peak District 106

MAP 208

EPILOGUE 210

GRADES 211

ACKNOWLEDGEMENTS 212

FOREWORD
BY DAN TURNER

Over the years, I have been lucky enough to travel to several well-known bouldering areas across the world. A special part of those adventures is meeting and connecting with people from far and wide. Naturally, people are interested to know where you are from and to hear about your local climbing area. Often, when you mention you are from Britain, after the usual comments about the weather, climbers from outside the UK unanimously think of the Peak District. Either reminiscing about their own experiences from times spent at the Stanage Plantation or referring to boulder problems and routes they have been exposed to from well-known films like *Hard Grit* or *The Real Thing*. On the one hand, it is always refreshing to hear people speaking passionately about UK climbing. On the other hand, there is always a part of me which wishes they knew about all the other amazing climbing opportunities the UK has on offer. I guess this was one of my motivations for creating *This is Yorkshire*, a short film which shone a light, albeit a small one, on my local area at the time. An attempt to document some of the beautiful boulders, the unique landscapes in which they exist and the communities that operated around them.

I guess *This Is Yorkshire* was the first time some of those boulders had been captured on film, bringing to life forgotten or overlooked gems hiding in the secluded dales of Yorkshire. Today, it is rare if you can't find a video of a boulder problem. Seemingly, every problem is documented and, within a blink of a second, hundreds of possibilities and options lie before us. All the while, stealing from us an opportunity to think and figure out the puzzles of rock which are presented to us. Unconsciously robbing us of an experience we never knew we could have. However, of all the rock types in the world,

I think grit is one of the few mediums which stands up against this modern culture. You cannot be taught the subtly of movement and body position from 6K, 240-frame-per-second ultra-slow-motion film; neither will it provide the patience required to master this rock type. In a way, grit is a great teacher; whether you are just starting out or an experienced rock dancer, there is something to discover and somehow days out on grit always provide an enriched and meaningful experience.

Thinking back to my most memorable climbing experiences, my thoughts regularly return to the days spent venturing out to gritstone boulders, perched proudly on the wild and windswept moors. I am continually drawn to big, beautiful lines, in remote locations. The kind of boulders which create natural sculptures that look like works of art. On first inspection, they look impossible. They take commitment and time to unravel the mysteries and sequences of the movement, until it becomes familiar and free. Where the little successes are sporadic but just frequent enough to keep you asking questions, even against the backdrop of frustration and failure. This process can often take whole seasons, even years, until you find the key that unlocks the gateway to success. Sometimes it never comes. Whatever the outcome, you build a relationship; you see your friend in different lights, from different angles and in different seasons. The fading purple of the rich heather moorlands marks the start. The calling of the grit. As life gradually retreats from the moors, we are presented with small windows of opportunity. Where crisp, cold days occasionally surface among the wild winds and rains of winter. Agonisingly, seemingly always aligning with times we are locked up, only left to stare out of a window, dreaming of

FOREWORD

what could have been. Over time the pressure mounts – time is running out – you start to notice the little white hats of cotton grass gently swaying in the wind against an ever more vibrant backdrop of emerging yellows in the hay meadows below. The solitary whistle of the curlew indicates time is nearly up. It's now our time to lie dormant, to think and prepare for our next opportunity.

Through this journey you begin to realise how extraordinarily lucky we are. Not only due to the incredibly unique circumstances by which these iconic boulders exist, but the access we have to them. Wrapped up in the moment – in the pursuit – it's sometimes easy to forget this. We are all guilty of becoming unconscious of our surroundings, the fragile environment in which we exist, as nature teeters in the background desperately trying to support all our needs. It takes thousands if not millions of years to create, but seconds to destroy. We must learn to look after our natural assets while respecting the wider community, appreciating their needs and priorities and finding some mutual ground, so we can continue to coexist in harmony and protect our valuable wild spaces for future generations to enjoy, just as we did.

This book is a beautiful reminder of what nature has created for us and Dave has captured this in a compelling way. I have only met Dave a few times, but I have always taken a keen interest in his photography. What has always struck me is the depth of his photos, the way he uses light and frames his images; he somehow manages to bring you into the moment, making you get a feel part of the image. Unsurprisingly, his passion comes through in this book and takes you on a voyage, expanding our horizons to the grit experience while also documenting the communities that help to build them. It makes you dream of the crisp winter days, scraping frost off your car window and knowing that the grit season is coming.

So, place this book somewhere which occasionally catches your eye, and acts as a spark of inspiration to go off and explore and create your own grit experience.

Approaching Gorple.

INTRODUCTION

It's funny the twists and turns life throws at you. For most of us, 2020 was a rather bizarre year unlike anything we'd ever experienced and, fingers crossed, unlike anything we'll experience again. So it was with some pleasure that late in 2020 I came across a copy of a French climbing book, in French, called *Bleau Blocs*. Here was just the sort of escapism I needed. Written and photographed by renowned Fontainebleau photographer Stéphan Denys, upon turning the pages I was transported back to the Forest instantly.

I could smell the pine trees and the pastries; I could imagine walking back to the car through the fading light of a Trois Pignons evening with sore skin and a feeling of supreme contentment. And all this was based on the strength of the photos alone, as I can barely read any French prose beyond spotting a few key nouns, the odd verb, and extrapolating the rest based on context (a key skill for any Brit abroad). It was a great relief that in the spring of 2021 Vertebrate published an English translation of *Bleau Blocs*. I could finally close my Google Translate browser tab. Little did I know that barely a year later I would be putting the finishing touches to a British counterpart to that book. But the seeds were well and truly sown.

In the UK we tend to live in the shadow of Fontainebleau bouldering. We borrow the French grading system, we even appropriate French climbing terms – arête, gaston, bloc – and the highest compliment we give to a boulder problem is to say it is 'Font-like'. So, the question that inevitably comes up in conversation between grit aficionados is: what does our native Pennine gritstone have that can compare with its sedimentary near neighbour, the sandstone of Fontainebleau? Can we even compete? And assuming we can hold our own, what does the best of the best on grit look like? Which guiding principles would lead us to the best? What would those 100 grit problems be? Messages were exchanged, lists were written and rewritten, spreadsheets were populated.

So here we are. *Grit Blocs* showcases 100 of the finest problems on the Pennines' gritstone outcrops, edges and even quarries. The words 'of the' are of key importance here because by no means is this a definitive list. The palette of gritstone bouldering is too rich to quantise into just 100 problems. It is a bit like building an epic sunset scene out of Lego bricks. You don't have enough different colours to do it justice but you can at least achieve a recognisable picture.

Which principles ended up guiding us to these problems? It might seem odd to impose rules on such an already difficult task but, as with any creative endeavour, limitations are key. Rules in this case are more like an imposed structure, without which we have no framework to work to, just as a musician might struggle without a beat, without rhythm.

Eventually, out of the fog of discussion, a working concept crystallised: non-eliminate up problems, without chipped holds, which must top out, on sound rock, the problems must be at venues that are accessible (i.e. not banned), and they must be legitimate boulder problems rather than routes or solos masquerading as problems. On top of this, a desire emerged to give a full account of gritstone bouldering across the grade range but also the stylistic spectrum. The high and the low, the old and the new, the well known and the esoteric, and the entire geographic spread. This, in theory, gives as full as possible a picture of the state of grit bouldering in the present day. Like all rules these have been bent on occasion,

INTRODUCTION

but not broken. However, I must offer a specific apology to fans of traverses – this isn't the book for you. Perhaps the next volume can be dedicated to the horizontal.

Another good reason to embrace the esoteric and look at the full range of climbing across the Pennines, not just Caley and Stanage, is because gritstone is not a medium which is frozen in time. Just as the wind and rain have shaped the rock into what we see today, humans are also capable of shaping the rock. Most obviously by quarrying, but also by chipping and vandalism. But more insidiously for climbers, we ourselves are capable of irreparably altering the rock by the very act of climbing. This is one of the main challenges we face today as gritstone climbers.

A universal truth we face is that entropy will take hold given half a chance. If we climb on gritstone which is wet or even just damp, we are damaging the rock. As we are already seeing at popular venues which actually have some fairly poor rock, like Stanage Plantation, it's usually a one-way street once the surface patina is compromised. Further to this, if we keep only climbing the same few problems that the social media algorithms amplify, if we submit to the commodification of climbing, just chasing soft-touch 'ticks' at a certain grade, then we're really putting a curse on the thing we love. Holds will get worn, landings will erode, and the soil will wash away. Certain problems have been left out of this book for that very reason, as indeed have entire crags.

None of us are perfect, but we can do better. We can spread the load wider, we can call out poor behaviour and educate each other, we can look after the rock, we can even pre-empt damage. We can wait until problems are actually dry, no matter how far we've driven or how psyched we are. 'Dry enough' to do the moves with a ton of chalk isn't dry enough to not be damaged. The ball is in our court with this one, and we're more than capable of making sure grit bouldering has a healthy future to add to its rich and varied history.

There is one crucial factor where gritstone can't compete with Fontainebleau, and never will. The Forest does have a rather unfair advantage in terms of density of climbing. In contrast, the problems in this book span a 140-mile stretch of upland from beyond Hadrian's Wall in the north all the way south past Matlock. To make matters worse, Stéphan Denys had a fifteen-year head start on the photography in comparison to my paltry quarter of a century of climbing on grit. However, our trump card is the huge number of talented climbing photographers we have in the UK. As a Sheffield-based photographer, a project like this is basically a dream job, and it's a privilege to be able to present my work alongside that of others with a similar affection for grit bouldering and an eye for a compelling image. Hopefully, between us we've done it justice.

Ned Feehally on *Ram Air*, Ramshaw Rocks.

GRITSTONE - BEHIND THE SCENES

If, like me, you've always regretted not spending more time exploring the climbing on offer in Scotland, or had the Lofoten Islands granite on your bucket list but never got round to going, then I have some good news for you. The tiny grains, pebbles and crystals making up the Pennine gritstone we climb on today originated in the rocks of mountains way to the north, from the granites of what are now Norway and the Cairngorms, around 300 million years ago.

It's a good job gritstone, and indeed climbers, didn't yet exist during the Carboniferous period, because decent conditions would have been hard to come by. Although it sometimes feels this way now in the middle of our humid climate-change summers, the UK was actually positioned down in the tropics, and a warm sea covered the north of England. Over countless years the mighty mountains in the distant north were laid siege to by the most innocuous and benign substance on the planet: water. Drip by drip, relentlessly the rain, snow and ice liberated tiny particles of rock and this water eventually unloaded its cargo in a huge river delta system.

Through the action of deposition this river delta eventually filled up the basin of this tropical sea, laying down sediment on top of the seabed, a seabed which would eventually become the limestone of the Pennines. We'll never know if it's just a coincidence that the limestone is below the gritstone both physically and in terms of climbing quality, as science doesn't have an answer for that. Geology does however give us some insight into how the genesis of the rock impacts directly on climbing.

One of the most recognisable characteristics of gritstone is horizontal bedding – giving rise to the break-to-break style of climbing and horizontal texture that dominates crags throughout the length of the Pennines. But why are some layers thick, others thin, and others show dramatic differences in texture? Why are hard layers atop softer layers which subsequently weather away to produce horizontal roofs and the steeply undercut bases of various crags?

The aforementioned river delta formed a complex and ever-changing system of swamps, channels, lagoons and streams. The local topography of such a delta is prone to dramatic change every time there is a big storm, a flood, a change in sea level, or simply a change in the type of sediment coming from upstream. Hence the horizontal bands of rock we see in grit mark changes in the delta – events in time recorded like the rings of a tree trunk.

The exact nature of the deposited material depends a lot on local factors. Generally speaking, faster streams and channels deposit larger grains and pebbles, with lower-energy areas giving rise to finer-grained deposits. Areas of softer rock, lacking the dissolved quartz to eventually glue it together solidly, form the sorts of caves and low roofs we recognise from the base of many crags. Smaller spots of softer material give rise to 'Huecos' and pockets. Where different speeds of flow occur in close proximity to each other, like where a fast channel abuts a shallow lagoon, we see huge changes in the resulting rock over a small area. Bear this in mind when visiting Simon's Seat and Hen Stones, where dramatically different rock occurs within a space of metres.

GRITSTONE – BEHIND THE SCENES

As fans of a sun-drenched evening session will note, the majority of gritstone edges face roughly west or south-west. The Pennines is formed of a broad anticline, a type of fold in the underlying rock. This makes most of the sedimentary layers of gritstone slant downwards to the east, and hence the rock generally comes to the surface facing west. This slant is plainly visible at many crags; a great place to observe this phenomenon is along the top of Stanage Edge, where the moor visibly and gracefully rolls away from the crag down towards Sheffield.

The eastward slant is shared by younger sandstone and coal-bearing layers east of the Pennines. The term Carboniferous comes from Latin, actually referring to the coal-bearing nature of the rock from this period. In more recent history this presence of coal, along with the gritstone, was a crucial factor in the North's role in the Industrial Revolution. Rock provided the energy source for industry, the building materials for towns and cities, and drove huge social and cultural changes which have shaped the north of England as we find it today.

Curbar Edge – where natural buttresses sit next to freestanding boulders and quarried bays.

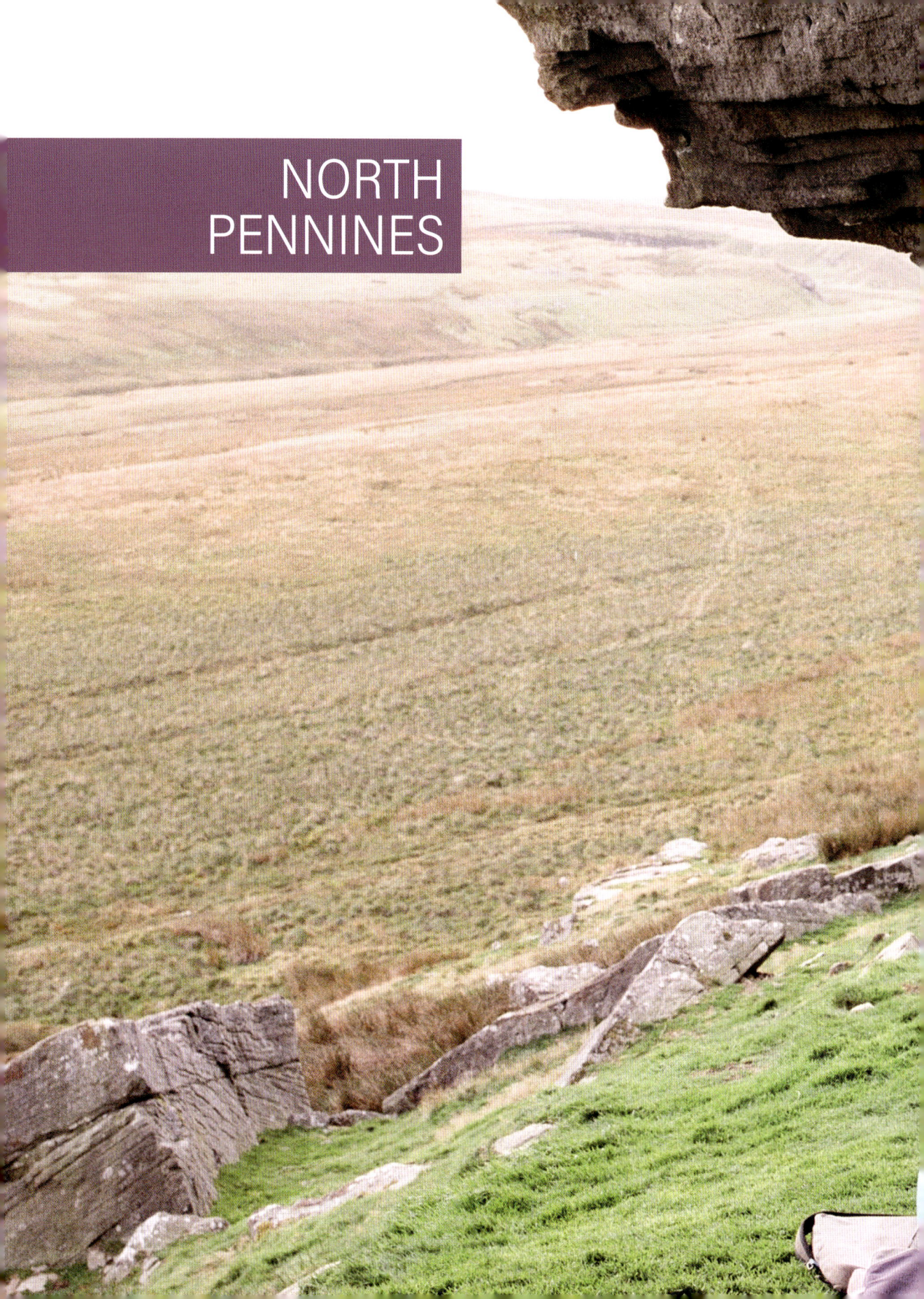

NORTH PENNINES

SHAFTOE CRAGS

 Blood Sport

Dan Turner sets up for (right), and latches (above), the big move to a distant fingertip edge. © Rowan Spear-Bulmer

NORTH PENNINES

We begin our journey through gritstone with the most northerly problem in this book. Shaftoe is distant from the main grit scene of the Pennines, although it's not actually the most northerly grit crag as Rothley sits four miles further north. Still, this is well and truly off the beaten track for most grit connoisseurs. We are eight and a half miles north of Hadrian's Wall here, only twenty-three miles from the Scottish border and well and truly in Northumberland. It's fair to say you're unlikely to bump into anyone nipping out for a quick after-work session from Leeds or Sheffield.

Shaftoe has suffered in the past from being a little oversold, leading to disappointed visitors turning up expecting a 'Fontainebleau of the North'. The climbing is scattered over the moor and rock quality is mixed, ranging from fairly poor and sandy in some places to very good, sound grit in others. This is not somewhere to climb unless the rock is absolutely one hundred per cent dry, but with care Shaftoe is a great venue to explore for a circuit, with some choice standout lines for the visitor.

Poking out from the hillside at the northern edge of the moor, Turtle Rock is as impressive a piece of Pennine grit architecture as any other. Solid rock, overhanging in every direction – it's a sight to behold. Various older problems skirt the fringes of this prow, but it wasn't until 2007 that Northumberland stalwart Andy Earl realised the potential of the underside of the Turtle's head, giving us *Blood Sport*. Huge moves on open-handed holds mark the way to gain the main horizontal break, from where just the 6a finish *Soft Centre* awaits. Just to the right, *The Boss* is a worthy 7b with a big move to the lip from the break. Elsewhere on the moor, *Purely Belter* remains a popular local classic, not least because the leaning rippled wall used to be given 8a. A good one for an ego boost, even if it is actually somewhere in the 7b or 7c range now.

GOLDSBOROUGH CARR

6a+ Jumping Jack Flash

It's fair to say County Durham's rock climbing is often overlooked as purely of interest to locals. Climbers traveling north up the A1 from Yorkshire or the Peak all too often skip over the county, making a beeline for the sandstone crags of Northumberland, and North East climbers tend to do likewise heading south. But Goldsborough Carr, with its remote feel, short solos, mid-grade highball walls and steep powerful roofs has more than earned its place alongside gritstone's more famous crags. Certainly there's enough to do here to earn a bag of chips in Barnard Castle afterwards, and that's the main thing.

Most of the crag is steeply undercut at its base, but at the right-hand end of Thin Wall Buttress the low roof expands into a full-height cave-like section. *Jumping Jack Flash* blasts out spectacularly from the edge of this cave, with big pulls

on generous holds, and is quite simply one of the most fun grade-6 problems on grit. Eminently photogenic and with a flat landing, it's one to feel like a complete hero on. Topping out is barely an inconvenience as it serves to delay your return to earth as a mere mortal. One more time for the camera? Just to the left, the companion problem *Thin Wall Special,* 5+, offers less spectacular but equally enjoyable moves up the short, flared crack.

Anyone operating at the higher grades will be able to enjoy *Jumping Jack Flash* once again as it forms the finish of both *Beth's Traverse* and *Holeshot*. These fingery and powerful lines out of the cave weigh in at 7b+ and 7c respectively, and with their small incut edges they are atypical for grit and require a bit of basic board strength. All those hours hanging off the fingerboard in your kitchen will not be wasted.

Adam Long on this spectacular North Pennines classic.

GOLDSBOROUGH CARR

7b+ George's Roof

On the huge low roof under the buttress of the previous problem is the modern classic *Second Coming*, 8b. This addition by Steve Dunning is one of the hardest problems of its type on grit, and succumbs only to a gymnastic feet-first approach to turning the lip. It is, however, beyond the pay grade of most of us. For a similarly full-bodied inverted experience at a more user-friendly grade, *George's Roof* is just the ticket.

Although a little higher and requiring a couple of pads and perhaps a spotter, *George's* is a fantastic set of involved moves through a roof on Thornbird Buttress. A throw from the back gains a big hold which strangely only feels good with feet high in the roof. It has perhaps suffered slightly by being variously described as having no particular finish, or being a drop-off-at-the-lip. But such a line deserves more than that indignity. A few different finishes are available, but the most logical and the safest-feeling is simply straight up the wall. The eventual finish topping out triumphantly on high jugs feels well earned.

The author eyes up the lip pocket. © John Coefield

YORKSHIRE

GREAT ROOVA

7a Aurora

Positioned high on the flanks of East Scrafton Moor, Great Roova occupies a commanding position overlooking Coverdale. No matter where you come from, it takes a long time to get to the parking spot on nerve-wracking single-track roads, and that's before you commence the half-hour uphill walk. As such, it really feels like the wild northern edge of Yorkshire gritstone bouldering, even though fans of Crag Willas some fifteen miles to the north will contend this is technically an inaccurate statement.

The jutting buttresses of Great Roova appear like battlements from the valley, rather like Wimberry in the Chew Valley, but as you approach, the more modest scale becomes evident until it's clear that the crag is actually well suited to bouldering and soloing, rather than an intimidating routes crag. The rock is fine grey grit echoing that of the Slipstones, just a few miles away as the crow flies over the other side of the moor. Although facing north, the sidewalls of the various protruding fins and buttresses, like the one taken by *Aurora*, face westwards, making a late spring evening session exploring the crag's various arêtes and faces an appealing option.

Aurora launches out across the prominent undercut fin from a very thin crimpy vertical edge, but, after a long move up to the left, bigger holds on a ramp-like flake come to hand, just as feet need to be built up to make the final move. The steep end face of the fin was taken by *Borealis* at 7c+, although at the time of writing a broken foothold puts that grade in jeopardy.

Rob Smith and the author on *Aurora* at the end of a long day.

SLIPSTONES

 Steve's Wall

Char Williams (above) and Steve Royle (right) savouring the commitment.

The Slipstones, while being very much in Yorkshire, managed to remain off the radar of the main Yorkshire grit scene for many years. The crag didn't even feature in the iconic 1998 YMC *Yorkshire Gritstone* guide, remaining the preserve of the North East guidebooks (covering the likes of the Teeside area, the North York Moors and County Durham), which weren't widely circulated. Hence the crag gained something of a reputation of a 'best kept secret' of Yorkshire gritstone for the locals who understood what a gem Slipstones is.

These days, however, the cat is well and truly out of the bag. Buttress after tall buttress of fine-grained grey grit; at first glance it's reminiscent of a sort of Burbage North made from Roaches Five Clouds rock. Slipstones sports a good number of what you could call legit non-highball boulder problems, especially towards the eastern end of the crag. But the majority of the climbing here – and arguably the best stuff – is on the short, mid-grade routes. Some you'd want a rack of gear for, some are outright solos with very poor landings, and some are approachable with bouldering pads, if only to allow a comfortable retreat. Pads or no pads, it's perhaps wise not to be lobbing off from the very tops.

At the far western end of the crag, on the final buttress, *Steve's Wall* is one of the best hybrid routes or highballs in that style, and a fantastic start to a day working your way rightwards along the crag, testing fingers, technique and head. Dating from 1982, Steve Brown probably couldn't have foreseen that we'd all be carrying huge foam mattresses up to the crag forty years later, although he probably had a good idea that his route would become to be regarded as something of a local classic. With a tricky start puzzling out the many blind scoops and dishes, the angle of the wall and some decent footholds thankfully mean you can afford to take your time and savour it. While the pads are down, just to the left *Paul's Arête* is equally classy – best climbed on the right to stay over the flat landing.

SLIPSTONES

7b+ Lay-by Arête

Having sung the praises of the highballs and the short solos at Slipstones, I should qualify those praises with a caveat. Although the solos outnumber non-highball boulder problems considerably, some of the latter are really superb and match up well against the best anywhere.

Although not graded as such at the time, local legend Paul Ingham's 1985 first ascent of *Lay-by Arête* – in inimitable 1980s lurid leggings of course – makes a strong claim to be one of the earliest 7b+ ascents on natural grit. Climbed the same year as John Allen's more well-known test piece *West Side Story* at Burbage, *Lay-by Arête* occupies the same niche locally: an outstanding, technical line on premium-quality rock, demanding clean technique, good conditions and strong fingers. Although traditionally graded English 6c in contrast to *West Side Story*'s 7a, there's not much to choose between them in difficulty, so maybe that's a touch of the traditionally harsh North East grading showing through.

Eighties climbers were famously a tough bunch, regularly risking sprained ankles or bruised heels from even the most innocuous falls. Modern day aspirants will be thankful of bouldering pads to take the sting out the repeated pivots off the arête, of which there are usually quite a few before success arrives, if indeed it does at all. Choose between a balancey layback or a heel or toehook on the starting crimp out to the right to check the barn-door as the right hand comes over to the arête. Once mastered, the good slot around to the left can be eliminated for a variation 'right-hand' 7c finish, although most will be content with a tick of the classic 7b+ version.

Char Williams opts for the frustrating heelhook solution.

GRIT BLOCS

SLIPSTONES

 ## Cypher

Above Ben Moon on the first ascent of *Cypher*. © Adam Long.   Right Kim Leyland on *Tiptoe*, one of the circuit of fantastic highballs hereabouts.

If there's one problem that really put Slipstones on the map nationally, then it's Ben Moon's desperate classic *Cypher*. Towering unhelpfully above the other problems at the eastern end of the crag, eminently photographable, it was a well-known project for some time. *Cypher* managed to hold all suitors at bay until 2002, and still ascents are relatively rare given the number of climbers operating at this grade currently, something the location can only partially account for.

Without a doubt it's one of the finest hard problems in the country, and yet actually quite atypical for gritstone – an arête with no arête climbing – with none of the usual ultra-technical grit weirdness here. Instead, it's surprisingly powerful and in-your-face to start, meaning most of us will just have to imagine how sweet it feels to finally nail the iconic ninja-kick move higher up.

Although overshadowed by *Voyager* and subsequently *Voyager Low Start* a few years later as Ben Moon's hardest contribution to gritstone bouldering, for many *Cypher* remains the cream of the crop; a unique combination of difficulty, line, setting, and rock quality. Stick this one on your bucket list – it's on mine.

BIRK GILL

7c+ The Lash

In terms of absolute standout bona fide classics, it has to be said there is a bit of a hole in Slipstones' repertoire between 7b+ and 8b. But it turns out that for all these years there has been a superb line just a few hundred metres away ready to fill that gap. It waited patiently until 2014 to be unlocked by Will Buck, and is undoubtedly one of the best finds in Yorkshire of the last decade.

Given how close it is to Slipstones, Birk Gill has a completely different character than its neighbour. We swap open moorland for a more sheltered situation in mature woodland, overlooking the gill bottom. Dropping in from the approach path gains a little shelter from the winter westerlies, and before long a sort of descending terrace in the hillside deposits you at the base of a big leaning wall.

An incredible system of writhing seams and dykes break out across the wall from the bottom left, arching across the face, just asking to be climbed.

The rock on *The Lash* is distinctly different to Slipstones, no silvery grey angular holds here. Instead, the vein system crosses a wall of slightly more fragile fine-grained grit, laced with iron deposits, almost reminiscent of the hardest fell sandstone of Northumberland. Flat crimps hidden in the ripples lead up right and build to a crescendo; an awkward stab into a pocket allowing a long final move for the ledge. A variation exists taking the pocket with the left hand leading to a rightwards exit, and a line just right again on the iron crimps, but thankfully neither detract from the main attraction.

Dan Turner (right; © Rowan Spear-Bulmer) and the author (left) adrift in a sea of ripples.

PANORAMA CRAG

 Phoenix Wall

James Parrott puzzling out the slab intricacies of *Phoenix Wall* (above and right) and *Make My Heart Fly* (centre).

It speaks well of the beauty of Yorkshire that it sports not one, not two, but three crags named Panorama. It sounds like a big claim, but the view over Pateley Bridge is worthy of the name. The little viewing platform you'll pass on the way in marks Panorama Crag as a popular local landmark, but in terms of bouldering *Phoenix Wall* is really the sole attraction here (pun intended). Although it has to be said the slabby *Goanna Arête* and *Lizard Wall* problems on the buttress just to the right are delightful, they are in no way adequate warm-ups for what awaits.

On this rough sweep of quarried grit, *Phoenix Wall* boils down to one very long move at the top. As we find time and time again, when a 7b+ is condensed into more or less one move, it's going to be a tough one. And when it's off vertical, expect at least to have to pull on some kind of grim, tiny hold, or a hard piece of footwork, or both. *Phoenix Wall* doesn't disappoint, with a thin matchstick crimp being basically your only handhold. Grit your teeth and choose between either a very high step and rockover, or otherwise a little bit of smearing alchemy and a quick pop might land you on the flatty, marking the end of difficulties.

For a completely different experience, nearby there are the moorland crags of Cow Close and Yeadon, a short drive from Panorama Crag. The views across Nidderdale are fantastic, the rock formations fascinating, and both venues really feel away from it all. The contrast in rock quality couldn't be more pronounced though, as the rock is some of the most fragile and sandiest you'll find on grit. The 5+ highball *Make My Heart Fly* at Yeadon is held back from classic status by the scrittley disintegrating nature of the rock, but if you can drop on it after a few dry weeks of being baked hard in the sun you might enjoy it, otherwise it's tough to recommend. Cow Close does sport a remarkable long, low bulging wall which boasts mantel after mantel: a pure-evil set of tricep-busting horror-show sloper mauling. Take a soft brush and plenty of ibuprofen.

GRIT BLOCS

BRIMHAM

 Successor State

Nowhere is the often-bizarre juxtaposition of climbers and the non-climbing public more obvious than at Brimham Rocks. Justifiably popular, Brimham's photogenic micro-landscape is a unique local landmark, now complete with a pay-and-display car park, toilets and cafe – all mod cons. For better or worse, there really isn't anywhere else quite like Brimham, and it has to be experienced.

Parallel with its identity as a tourist destination is Brimham's long history as a rich climbing spot. The various crags and pinnacles offer challenges across the grades. One of the aspects of this symbiosis is while the picnic tables may be full of tourists seeing away endless coffees and ice creams, yards away a climber could be quietly committing to a palm-sweating run-out finish to a trad route, or a necky solo.

The bouldering at Brimham often requires a similarly singular focus. There's plenty of good problems on decent rock of normal bouldering height, like the classic groove of *Whisky Galore* for example. But arguably the finest problems here, on the best rock, are those which bridge the gap between boulder problem and solo. The classic highball walls, ribs and arêtes, along with the more modern, harder highballs. It's on these challenges where nothing punctures the concentration bubble more abruptly than a kid walking around the corner and loudly exclaiming: 'Mum, what they doing up there wi' no ropes? They're gonna fall off – look!'.

Successor State is one of the finest highball arêtes at Brimham. First climbed in 1986, it's a serious undertaking as a pure solo but one undergoing something of a renaissance thanks to bouldering pads and judicious use of a spotter to deal with the landing. A tricky start to turn the bulge leads to a comfortable standing position before committing to the top. Maybe too comfortable if anything, giving plenty of chances to talk yourself out of it. Just be sure to save a little juice in the tank for the very top, as there are no straws to clutch at after the final, good face hold. Be pleased with yourself strutting back to the car through the crowds. They don't know, and it's probably for the best that they don't. That feeling is just for you.

Top and right The arête moves lead James Parrott to a brief respite before the top-out. **Above** The author on the more sedate *Whisky Galore*.

CROW CRAG

7c Fluide

Barely a mile from the fleshpots of Brimham lies Crow Crag. Tucked away in the woods, this is home to a problem that's established itself as one of the best short wall problems in Yorkshire – a modern esoteric classic.

Parallel thin cracks lead easily enough to a high thin undercut, where things quickly turn powerful as the holds run out and the wall steepens slightly. There are no options to puzzle out, no maze of intermediates to navigate, no sequence of blind alleys to waste time on. All that remains is one very stern lurch for the top, unwinding, powering through the feet to full stretch. Or for the unlucky short, a dyno. Either way, the aim is to drop the right hand on to the top hold just at the apex of the trajectory. Judge it wrongly and you'll be flying outwards from the rock too far, or too close in for the footholds to stick properly.

As is so often the case with undercuts, it doesn't actually feel good until you've passed it and landed the final hold. Easy when it works, desperate on every other attempt? We shouldn't expect anything less on a one-move 7c on grit, really.

The start (centre; © **James Turnbull**), the set-up (left; © **John Coefield**) and the execution (right; © **Oliver Parkinson**) of the crux of *Fluide*, demonstrated by Will Buck, Kim Leyland and Oliver Parkinson respectively.

NOUGHT BANK - GUISECLIFF

7a+ Trust

The name is apposite in more ways than one: when arriving on a dull autumn day it's difficult to believe that in the jumble of boulders above the hairpins of the Nought Bank Road there lies a sublime gritstone arête. As you sweatily drag your pads up the hill through the undergrowth, a little trust is required to believe you will find a clean problem.

The encroaching tree cover ensures the slabby side of the arête is indeed fairly dirty; however, curiously, after leaving the initial left-hand sidepull all the key holds lie in a cleaned strip about fifteen centimetres wide along the arête itself. This at least keeps you honest; no temptation to start clutching for straws on the slab!

Leaning away unhelpfully to the right, the arête feels surprisingly big in the hand, yet the potential to barn-door off is constant. A battle with geometry more than gravity – after all it's only really gravity which is keeping you on in the first place. Clean smearing technique, heels low, with the problem name always in mind, should bring the generously chunky final arête holds to hand and a smile to your face.

The rest of the hillside at Nought Bank bears plenty of other fruit for the boulderer, when clean and in condition. *A Little Sparkle*, a 7a slab with a dynamic finish comes in for well-deserved praise. But while your pads are under *Trust* don't miss the complete contrast of trying the arête from a sit start on the other side. Supposedly Font 6c, the difficulties are short lived but, *Trust* me, it feels harder.

James Parrott and Lawrence Cooper unlock *Trust* (centre and right), and the frustrating other-side sit start *Little Faith* (left).

GRIT BLOCS

HIGH CRAG - GUISECLIFF

 Snaketongue Truffleclub

James Parrott on the unique iron edges on *Snaketongue Truffleclub* (right) and the delightful solitude of *Mr Incredible* at Rowantree Tor (above).

Brimham Rocks is well known for its unusual rock formations, including the spectacle of big bulging boulders seemingly supported by almost nothing. With softer supporting rock scoured away by millions of years of wind and rain, these can almost look like mushrooms dotting the moorland. As luck would have it, such formations are not exclusively the domain of Brimham, and one such mushroom lies across Nidderdale at High Crag, Guisecliff.

Snaketongue Truffleclub takes the side wall of this particular fungus from sitting, using a remarkable set of iron crimps, forming the edge of huge plates of seemingly bulletproof patina atop the softer rock beneath. Steely fingers are required, leading to a final flick to a big hold and straightforward top-out. If fingers weren't warmed up beforehand, then they certainly will be now.

Visible on the other side of the road on the opposite side of Heyshaw Moor lies Rowantree Tor. Tucked away past the shooting lodge at the top of a hidden valley, the crag has a great little set of problems on good compact rock in a delightfully quiet spot. Combined with High Crag this offers a great afternoon of climbing in the low to mid grades away from the crowds – a fine alternative to the tourist circus at Brimham.

BRANDRITH

7c Heaven in Your Hands

Prior to 2004, the mention of a crag called Brandrith would probably be met with a bemused shrug or a blank look from most boulderers. All that changed however when Dave Sutcliffe made the first ascent of the justifiably named *Heaven in Your Hands*. An incredible line up the gently leaning left-hand arête of a slim pillar on superb rock, it was immediately clear this was something a bit special. Over the years since, it's proved to be a highly-prized problem, one of the finest problems in the mid-to-high 7s in Yorkshire if not the entire UK. The right-hand arête of the pillar makes a good stab at greatness, but the landing is something of a killjoy. Although there is a limited circuit of other problems, *Heaven in Your Hands* is undeniably the main draw in terms of bouldering – at least the rest of us know the crag exists now.

Sitting on a small patch of moorland south of Thruscross Reservoir, Brandrith faces north so gets little if any sunlight in winter and with the right breeze can give decent conditions well into the warmer months. A choice of technical and intricate sequences on pinchy arête slopers and undercuts, with a heelhook or two, should unlock the long move way up on the right to a lone, poor edge. From here it's just a couple more moves – should be easy if you can hold it all together, right? Anyone too short to reach the edge might consider it was originally climbed entirely on the arête, so there is hope yet, although that might feel a lot more like the original grade of 7c+.

Dave Sutcliffe on the first ascent (left; © **Dave Sutcliffe**). The author (centre) and Dan Varian (right; © **Adam Long**) tussle with the technical intricacies.

THRUSCROSS

 ## Damnation

A real taste of Yorkshire esoterica, downstream of Thruscross Reservoir in the Washburn Valley lies a little compact rib of premium gritstone. With a reputation for hard-to-find problems, and epic bracken-bashing required, the bouldering at Thruscross is a dish best enjoyed by those with an appetite for plenty of legwork and exploration. However, *Damnation* enjoys relatively simple access; the main limiting factor is lingering dampness due to the vegetation.

Unlocked by Dave Barrans in 2017, hiding away in the densely wooded western side of the valley, it seems a little jarring to be getting to grips with rounded subtle slopers in the shadow of the brutal concrete structure of the dam. But like most grit arêtes, a brutal approach to climbing is only likely to bring frustration. A breeze, dry conditions, trust in friction for both hands and feet, a bit of power and a bit of that grit 'feel' should go a long way.

Rob Smith tries to milk every last drop of friction from the Cratcliffe-esque grit.

FLASBY FELL

8a+ Rhythm

Usually when you stagger in to a remote boulder, exhausted and pouring with sweat having dutifully followed the guidebook approach yet somehow ended up thrashing for an hour through waist-high bracken carrying a ton of pads, normal practice is to curse heavily and be generally less than complimentary about the quality of the climbing you've expended a full day's worth of energy simply walking to. Or at least that's what this author usually does. However, lines like *Rhythm* are simply too good to stay in a bad mood about for very long.

Originally given 8b, this modern classic from Steve Dunning follows a compelling rampline, after which the difficulty kicks up a few gears. A positive backhand edge and small pocket theoretically allows access to the sublime slopers over the lip, some classic gritstone tussling, and hence victory. Expect to have an extremely hard time in anything other than mint conditions, as the problem catches a lot of sun. At the time of the first ascent in the early 2000s, *Rhythm* was one of the few problems in the country on grit claiming the magical grade of 8b and, although the grade has settled at 8a+, the quality of the experience has not diminished, and it remains one of the most sought-after problems at the grade.

In contrast to the crags on the neighbouring fells – Crookrise, Eastby – the rock on Flasby's Lone Boulder is not the fine grey gritstone you might expect, but instead a coarser, more-rounded variety more reminiscent of the rock in Staffordshire, some sixty miles to the south. The slight pink tinge is of course amplified as the boulder catches the last light of the day and, successful ascent or not, there can be few better places to enjoy a sunset.

Will Buck on *Rhythm* (above; © James Turnbull) and the neighbouring *Sugar Shack*, 8a (left; © James Turnbull).

RYLSTONE

 Molly Moocher

Rylstone is known for being very spread out, with long walks being an essential part of the experience. However, this modern classic is situated at a comparatively roadside thirty-five-minute uphill stroll, so there's no excuse really.

Taking the left-hand arête on a boulder beneath the initial section of crag topped with the iconic Rylstone cross, *Molly Moocher* had to wait until 2009 to receive a first ascent from visiting Peak raider Jon Fullwood. Once again demonstrating that even at well-known spots it's never safe to assume everything of value has already been done years ago.

The sit start is 7b+ and makes use of a remarkable vertical slot to start with, before gaining the arête and hence the stand-up line. The big slot seems to have other slots within it, a sort of Russian doll of grit pockets. You'd swear it was chipped, except chisels can't go around corners, so this one is just a marvel of nature.

The first ascentionist on his own problem. © **John Coefield**

RYLSTONE

8b **Lanny Bassham**

A boulder to stop you in your tracks, if ever there was one. Truly one of the most beautiful pieces of gritstone: rough, massive, and visible for miles around. Even if you don't climb 8b, and let's face it most of us don't, it's worth the walk just to behold the monumental audacity of the line. If this doesn't set the imagination racing, then check for a pulse.

The huge *Cocoa Team Special* boulder seems to be cleaved right through by the crack of its namesake problem, like a split coconut. Appearing out of the mist on a dank day, dark and resembling some sort of unhelpfully rounded-off cube, it's an intimidating spectacle. The broad, open arête of *Lanny Bassham* is only just climbable. The term 'arête' is unhelpful really; it lacks anything arête-like you might be able to grab hold of and seems to defy geometry by overhanging in about five different directions at once. Fortitude has provided just enough pockets and a decent landing, but it's still droppable right to the very top.

Despite being an obvious challenge, it still held out until 2009 – and alarm bells are always ringing when something takes Ben Bransby multiple visits. When one of the most talented climbers of his generation has a big project, you know it's going to be something a bit special, and *Lanny Bassham* doesn't disappoint. You'll need winning to be in body as well as mind for this one.

Ben Bransby on perhaps his finest contribution to gritstone. © Adam Long

RYLSTONE

6b Poetry in Motion

It's not all completely desperate hero fodder up at the northern end of Rylstone, you'll be glad to discover. Gritstone has no shortage of grandiosely named pieces of climbing, but this is really one which lives up to the name.

The tall, slabby arête, exquisitely sculpted by thousands of years of wind and rain, offers a series of ripples, scoops and slopers on perfect rock heading skyward. All too soon these terminate at a literal bucket, sparing us too much of an ordeal to top out. It's a shame the arête doesn't continue on for twenty-five metres, so all that remains is the task of standing up into the bucket to finish. One of the best at the grade. The delicate slab immediately to the right of the arête, above a sloping landing, is *The White Doe*, with a similar bucket groove finish arriving just in time. Both superb and worth the forty-five-minute walk-in.

Right Ben Bransby enjoying grit perfection. © **Adam Long**

YORKSHIRE

GRIT BLOCS

CROOKSTONES

 ## Greg's Arête Right

Well worth the walk; Rob Smith (above) and the author (right) in contrasting conditions.

Facing north-west, in a position overlooking a steep gully, the jumble of blocks and arêtes of Crookstones suffers from a veil of green during the cold and damp months, and is largely overshadowed by its more prestigious neighbour Rylstone, with which it shares an approach. However, it's very much worth a look for the boulderer seeking a few quiet gems. Offering a bit of morning shade in summer, and even in the depths of winter, the fine face of *Greg's Wall* faces west and hence is grey and clean and so is a viable proposition year round.

It's the left-hand arête of this wall which brings us here. Climbed on its clean right-hand side, it's a little marvel of Font 4+. Unlike many grit problems at the lower end of the grade scale which lack a distinct line or purpose, this compelling arête feels and climbs exactly like a harder problem, except with better hand and footholds. The arête itself is beautifully grippy and just about stays clear of scrittle, the pockets on the face are reassuring, and the top is angular, with ample footholds, yet competent technique is required. You're on a gritstone arête after all, so sloppy footwork can still be punished! The only fly in the ointment is the block in the landing, but it's easily padable. It's a shame low-grade problems can't all be this good.

CROOKRISE

Jason's Roof

Jason Myers really was on fire in the mid-1990s. Having made the now legendary first ascent of *Brad Pit* at Stanage in 1995, he swooped on some major Yorkshire plums the following year. Crookrise is one of the finest jewels in the Yorkshire grit crown, with routes full of history and bold technical classics across the grade spread, and an incredibly varied range of bouldering from stand-alone blocks to start-of-a-route type problems. With the addition of *Jason's Roof* in 1996, Myers showed us once again how he was operating really quite far ahead of his time.

A quarter of a century later and this problem remains a much lusted-after classic, and one whose very modern steep physical style stood out as visionary at the time of the first ascent. Wildly steep and tackled by full-bodied heelhooking, compression and upside-down slapping, in retrospect this was an early marker of what would become the defining modern bouldering style. Had it been at Burbage instead of Crookrise it would probably have got more of a well-deservéd fanfare at the time.

Once the aforementioned sequence is successfully executed to the very welcome jug at the lip, it's just a matter of turning the lip to bask in glory on the upper slab. No top-out, no tick, I'm afraid. If this all proves too easy then the neighbouring *Sideliner*, 8a, is only just getting the attention it deserves. A more recent hard classic on the boulders beneath the crag is *Sole Fusion*, an 8a from the prolific Dave Sutcliffe, this time a very different proposition to *Jason's Roof*. Bring as many pads as you can muster and a bucket full of commitment for the top.

Oliver Parkinson (left; © **Oliver Parkinson**) and Neil Mawson (above; © **Adam Long**) in the grip of this steep classic.

CROOKRISE

7a+ Ron's Crack II

Legally speaking, the British Mountaineering Council owns Crookrise crag, having purchased it in 2017. Although another way of looking at it is that they are merely custodians of the crag, awaiting the day that Ron Fawcett returns and wants to take the crag home with him, because in every other sense Big Ron owns Crookrise.

Imagine for a minute you are a young Ron Fawcett, growing up in Embsay and equipped with ample climbing ability, a cool head, and a crag to yourself most of the time. What a time to be alive! Ron's contributions to the history of Crookrise are too numerous to list, and today two standout crack boulder problems bear his name. This is one of the rare instances where the sequel eclipses the original, like *Terminator 2*.

For *Ron's Crack II* you will need your clothes, your boots, and your motorcycle. Well, a couple of pads will be of more use than the bike if we're honest. And if you can rustle up a spotter on the rocks to the right, you'll be happier. Big, physical moves, surprisingly so for a mid-1970s trad route, lead to the crack proper, crossing the hanging shield-like headwall. Most will take it with the left hand only, but masochists are free to fingerlock their way up if desired. Either way, it's an absolutely brilliant intimidating finale, so channel that nineteen-years-old-Ron-Fawcett energy and go for it.

Adam Long gets stuck into *Ron's* (right; © **John Coefield**), while John Coefield discovers the vertical techy moves of *Diet Pepsi* (above).

EASTBY

7c+ Ill Gotten Gains

It's funny how certain lines and certain problems go through a journey, finding their identity and their level, in much the same way we as climbers and as human beings do. *Ill Gotten Gains* feels like it's just emerged from adolescence, and is now reaching maturity.

A well-known project, the attractive rampline to the right of *Knuckle Slab* was originally climbed by Steve Dunning, and graded 8a+. The line has subsequently lost a huge pebble, which hence removed any possibility of reaching a limb to the arête, and so became completely independent. Then as the line gained popularity and more ascents came, the sequence was further refined, so the groove can be backhanded instead of having to really crank on the grim crimp; it is likely in the 7c/7c+ range.

Somewhat paradoxically, as the line shifted to be more direct, the grade has gone down. If this shows us anything, it's that grades are a nonsense at the best of times! But it's easy to forget that climbing and grading an unclimbed line is a completely different ball game from making a repeat of a problem which already carries a grade. Add in a whole host of online videos and some sort of collective morphic resonance takes over and grades of new problems can and do often drop.

For *Ill Gotten Gains* it feels the problem will settle down now, but who knows what further improvements can be found? One thing is for sure: when you stand beneath that immaculate fine grey rampline, in the winter dusk light, waiting for that one final good attempt before it gets dark, you can forget all about grades. You'll either climb it or you won't, and that's all there is to it.

Sometimes the subtlest of adjustments to body position make all the difference. John Coefield makes the most of the coldest of winter conditions.

SIMON'S SEAT

7b+ Victoria's Secret

I don't know who Simon was, but he had impeccable taste in furniture. The summit of Barden Fell, dotted with gritstone outcrops, is a truly remarkable spot to climb at. No matter what approach you take, you're looking at over 200 metres of ascent to reach Simon's Seat, and duly the views in all directions are expansive. In summer, the breeze, exposed position and ample north-facing options can be your saviour against soaring temperatures and the ever-present midge threat. In winter, with the meagre few hours of low sunlight raking across the moor, the friction high, the air crystal clear and the relentless wind biting keenly into any exposed flesh, it offers an exhausting but absolutely unforgettable day out. The incongruous spectacle of a decorated Christmas tree is an additional winter bonus. Best coupled with a visit to nearby Lord's Seat, Hen Stones and, if daylight permits, Earl's Seat for the full Barden Fell experience.

Being primarily a routes crag it's no surprise that many of the best problems at Simon's Seat are highball, so it's best savoured with a group of friends, a few pads and a cool head. The remarkable, tall, mid-grade highballs of *And She Was* and *I'll Bet She Does* are justifiably popular, taking lines up an incredible narrow pillar of grit dotted with rugosities ranging from slopey humps to baked-potato-sized doorknobs. The E3 grade for both is more useful than any bouldering grade if we're being honest, as above half height you are in soloing territory.

Although not as high, the recently realised potential of the rib to the left of *Victorian Climb* still demands commitment for the top-out. Don't expect an especially easy ride on the leaning lower arête beautifully peppered with slopey scoops, pockets and protrusions. Dan Mitchell-Garnett's *Victoria's Secret* is up there with the best lines discovered on Yorkshire grit in recent years.

Dan Mitchell-Garnett on the first ascent (left; © **Elis Rees**) and Oliver Parkinson on an early repeat of this proud line (above; © **Oliver Parkinson**).

LORD'S SEAT

McNab

Second stop on the Barden Fell tour, only a short trip across the flagged path, Lord's Seat is smaller in stature than Simon's Seat but if anything is an even better bouldering spot. Once again, it offers shadier, steeper problems for the warmer months, and a few south-facing gems to soak up what little winter sunlight is available. Despite being only 500 metres from Simon's, the rock feels very different; gone are the pockets and protruding nuggets, replaced with good rough grit slopers, with just a hint of finely spaced horizontal bedding. Although high challenges exist, it feels very much a more relaxing place to climb for the pure boulderer. The crag still doesn't scrimp on the views though, as now you can see well into the distance to the south-east, to the radar domes of Menwith Hill and beyond.

Taking centre stage at Wall Buttress, the *McNab* block has a couple of good problems on its right flank, but the bulging rounded line up front of the prow is inescapably the showpiece problem here. Pulling on from standing on the rock plinth sets you off into a brilliant sequence of powerful squeezy moves, gaining a high undercut overlap and maintaining the tension, while a delicate foot swap allows you to turn the bulge and quest on to the top. The sit start at 7b+/7c adds another couple of powerful moves into, and out of, a high undercut, this time with the right hand, then dig deep to battle through the top again. Superb.

On a premium winter's day, Louise Hall embarks with careful footwork (right) and Laurence Everitt keeps it together for the top section (left).

HEN STONES

 7a+ **Bird Flu**

A mere few hundred metres' stagger through the heather from either Simon's or Lord's Seat and once again the character of the rock changes completely. Hen Stones doesn't actually offer much climbable rock at all, but what it does offer is extraordinary. Contrasting starkly with the dark earth, the platinum-grey rocks and boulders that are strewn all around the main block make the venue reminiscent of the many World War II aircraft crash sites dotted around the Pennines. Raw, espresso-black surface peat is dotted not with tangled sun-bleached aluminium, but with some of the finest silvery gritstone imaginable. Almost fluorescing in the fading light of a winter sunset, with texture under the fingers like caster sugar, it has a rare, fragile beauty.

Slightly sheltered from cold winter northwesterlies and the ideal height for bouldering, it couldn't be a more perfect end to a day on Barden Fell. Climbed on the left-hand side, *Hen Arête* makes a justifiable claim to be the best problem here, but with the neighbouring crack tantalisingly close to hand, purists will prefer the right-hand side, *Bird Flu*. With no blinkers required, only the arête, a sloper and a few tantalising micro-ripples for feet to aim for, the grade may be debatable, but the quality of the line is not.

It's worth reiterating here a point we'll return to time and time again, and that is to not climb on wet or damp gritstone. Problems like these are enormously prone to damage if attempted when not absolutely dry – the surface texture is close to Northumbrian sandstone, with all that brings with it. Tread lightly.

The author in the dying last light of midwinter.

HUNTER'S STONES

7c Hunter's Roof

It's funny how little details can transport you somewhere else. Visiting *Hunter's Roof* on an autumn day, it's hard not to somehow be reminded of Fontainebleau – the smell of the pine trees, the yellowing needles scattered atop the boulders, the orange leaves carpeting the car parks, and the labyrinth of paths to find the actual problem. Those *pignon* hills you get in the Forest with maybe a boulder or two on top, a hidden classic. It's easy to forget that none of the trees were actually here when this problem was first climbed.

This Fontainebleau hallucination does require a little suspension of disbelief on the part of the visitor. Firstly, instead of beautifully smooth Fontainebleau sandstone, we have some of the roughest gritstone imaginable. Any coarser and it would be virtually unclimbable. As it is, it's just about manageable, but you'd be advised not to have too many attempts, and make sure to wait for decent conditions. It would be easy to write off *Hunter's Roof* on this basis alone if the line wasn't so compelling, and the movement not up there with the best on grit or sandstone.

The other bit of heavy lifting we require the imagination to do is in ignoring the huge microwave communication antenna at the top of the hill. Originally part of the country's Cold War-era long-distance radio network, it was designed to keep running in the aftermath of nuclear attacks. You can see why this site was chosen for this line-of-sight network, as the views from the top, if you can peer over the trees, are vast. The commanding bulk of Almscliff can clearly be seen, and if you squint, on a clear day, I'm pretty sure you can see Cuvier Rempart.

The author being torn to ribbons but secretly enjoying it.

GRIT BLOCS

ALMSCLIFF

6b Flying Arête

The focal point for Yorkshire bouldering, Almscliff is one of the most well-developed crags in the county. Visible from miles away, a rich history, quick to access from Leeds and with a utilitarian function in being one of the fastest-drying crags imaginable, there's no wonder it's popular. And with that comes the development of the crag as something of a shrine to hard moves for hard moves' sake – traverses, eliminates, linkups. Local enthusiasts getting creative to eke extra value out of seemingly worked-out rock. In that sense, Almscliff sits in the same niche that places like the Bowderstone, Raven Tor and Parisella's Cave occupy in their respective local scenes. Almscliff has a trump card though: its own curiously unique brand of gritstone that doesn't really seem to exist anywhere else.

But I'll let you into a secret – the best problems at Almscliff are actually the lower- to mid-grade natural lines. *Flying Arête* is a favourite, a striking line you just can't walk past, but the right-hand arête of the same block is also worthwhile. Similarly, *Matterhorn Ridge, Pork Chop Slab, Patta's Arête, Morrell's Wall, Hanging Rib* – to name a few – are all excellent in their own right, and together form a brilliant circuit of varied climbing, but each one unmistakably Almscliff.

A classy high point of the Almscliff mid-grade circuit, Frances Bensley moves along this fine rising arête.

GRIT BLOCS

ALMSCLIFF

6c+ **Syrett's Roof**

For the local repeat visitor, Almscliff bouldering is really all about the roofs, small crimps and the steep stuff. *The Keel* and all its variations, *Matt's Roof*, *Jess's Roof*, and the *Demon Wall Roof* problems with endless linkups. Aesthetic considerations can be sidestepped, the utility of the fast-drying, accessible rock and the sheer number of hard variations packed into one place mean arguably that Almscliff is one of the best locals' crags imaginable and, like all good locals' crags, it repays persistence.

However, The 'Cliff does have one or two roofs up its sleeve to delight the visitor looking for a fast-drying, natural line untarnished by chips or rules on which to refine one's skills. *Syrett's Roof*, from 1972, is one of the best. A superb example of an essential skill in anyone's gritstone repertoire – the committing rockover around a roof lip, at a slightly uncomfortable height. One which, when mastered, pays dividends as it will crop up time and time again over the course of a grit climbing career.

In the case of *Syrett's*, as always seems to be the situation, the handholds aren't quite positive enough to inspire confidence, and it's too high up for anyone in antiquity to have chipped a convenient bucket hold. Once committed, the reach seems long, and the holds aimed for aren't that positive either, so keep pushing and willing your weight up and on to the right foot (hint – consciously moving your arse over your foot helps) until beyond that crucial tipping point. Although a touch airy, the landing isn't too much of a punisher, thankfully.

Laura Smitton (right; © **Adam Long**) and Frances Bensley (left and above) get to grips with *Syrett's* in different light.

CALEY

 Ben's Groove

The other half of the Wharfedale bouldering binary star, the yin to Almscliff's yang, Caley remains an essential venue. The encroaching greenness does nothing to decrease the popularity – is this the penalty for improved air quality? Neither does the often-frustrating business of obtaining genuinely good conditions at this north-facing crag put off suitors to the crag's many classy lines. However you look at Caley, it's diametrically opposed to Almscliff in almost every way, but it's in partnership that the two are greater than the sum of their parts. It's no surprise that the two form a killer local combination for Leeds climbers.

One of the most un-Almscliff problems, and one of Caley's most sought after, is *Ben's Groove*. The slopey tussle above a not-beyond-question landing to access the committing rockover into the upper slabby groove lingers long in the memory. But for many the stand-up problem is merely a gateway drug leading inevitably to locking horns with the powerful, yet technical, sit start moves up the fantastic lower groove. Clean footwork and an ability to hold it together are prerequisites. Amusingly, folklore states that three suitors to the sit start made presumed first ascents all on the same day, oblivious to each other. Incredible scenes.

Oliver Parkinson (left; © **Oliver Parkinson**) and Sam Pratt (right; © **Sam Pratt**) with handfuls of Caley's finest. John Coefield (centre; © **Adam Long**) commits to the rockover to access the upper slab and hence glory.

CALEY

 ## High Fidelity

A glaringly obvious Last Great Problem of Yorkshire grit for some time, Steve Dunning's 2003 first ascent of *High Fidelity* is something of a high-water mark of that golden age of early noughties bouldering. Baggy skate trousers, thin pads, scarcely a beard in sight and no fingerboards at the crag. Good times.

Coming a year later than Ben Moon's *Cypher* at Slipstones, arguably this is a bigger all-round test of bouldering ability, and at a height too. The weird rotation into and then out of the undercut at half height might be the technical crux, but the long pop into the good pocket high up remains a heart-breaker. It's still relatively rarely repeated even now – a true bucket-list problem for any hard, modern boulderer. One of the best lines anywhere, one of the biggest boulders, and one of the hardest, and at one of the most iconic Yorkshire bouldering crags. It's a tough combination to beat.

North East legend Andy Earl on an early repeat of *High Fidelity* (right; © **Darren Stevenson**).

Another unmissable hard classic is *Zoo York*, (centre; climber Pete Dawson) and meanwhile lower-grade lines like *Forked Lightning Crack* (left; climber John Coefield) haven't lost their charms.

THE CHEVIN

 ## The Geminid Trail

In the woods of Otley Chevin, the long diagonal face of the Satellite boulder is something of a tribute to Alpine granite, offering hard direct brutal lines on small holds in the truest Ticino style. A remarkable block of gritstone, it remained undiscovered by climbers until 2014, which is incredible given that it's clearly visible from a well-used footpath a stone's throw from established venues. Just goes to show what gems are out there still to be discovered.

On the transition between the steep and slabby faces, *The Geminid Trail* offers a quality set of powerful yet subtle moves, relatively accessible, and at the time of writing just about manages to stay clear of the encroaching moss. Nature is often quick to take back the boulders that we temporarily borrow, and the Satellite is one where this is an especially rapid process.

The author amid the ferns and moss of The Chevin.

THE CHEVIN

8a+ Brownian Motion

Whereas the style of climbing on the Satellite boulder is a nod to Switzerland, at the other end of The Chevin the boulders scattered in the vicinity of *Brownian Motion* are somehow reminiscent of Fontainebleau.

This is a notion that we return to time and time again, living in the shadow of Fontainebleau bouldering as we do in the UK. To compare a boulder or venue to Font is the highest compliment. But at The Chevin that is not to say that they actually look like Font boulders, or climb like Font boulders, because they don't really. Unlike *Hunter's Roof*, it's not as obvious as being some rocks on a hilltop surrounded by pine trees. It might instead be something to do with the carpet of recently fallen leaves, the layout of the boulders, or maybe the little square face of the free-standing block packed with mid-grade problems. Fontainebleau venues certainly don't sport as many improvised rope swings as The Chevin, but arriving on a cold dry winter's morning there's definitely something to remind you of the Forest. It's subtle but it's there; trust me.

And you'll want those cool dry winter conditions for *Brownian Motion*. The big wall looming over the warm-up boulder makes an instant impression. The premium rock quality is evident, with sweeping micro-feathers etched on the upper wall, making way to rounded slopers higher up. Tall and uncompromising and, like *Ill Gotten Gains* further north, this was originally done with a distant toehook on the arête. Originally given 7c+ by Andy Brown, before being later reclimbed without recourse to the arête by Martin Smith at the current grade.

Truth be told, only the very lankiest can probably reach the arête anyway, but still the current solution does feel a little purer and arguably more satisfying. The final few moves are on fine fingertip slopers, but gaining access to these is a long hard pull off a little nugget-like right-hand crimp. It has a bit of an angular edge to it, a sort of rugosity a bit like … hang on a minute … a bit like those *gratton* crimps in Fontainebleau. Mystery solved.

John Coefield on one of the great neighbouring easier lines (bottom). Close but no cigar for the author on the main event (top and right; © John Coefield).

GRIT BLOCS

ILKLEY

 Frank

Ilkley is a crag of contrasts. Rob Smith on the fine-grained unblemished *Frank* (top and right).

As an iconic location dripping in Yorkshire cultural baggage, Ilkley requires no introduction. The Cow and Calf are instantly recognisable, merely yards from the cafe and very close to the town of Ilkley itself – this is an extremely popular spot with the general public, with all that comes with it. Aside from the obvious downsides, one unfortunate aspect of the popularity and accessibility of Ilkley is the proliferation of chipped holds, a sad legacy from when the boundaries of acceptability in climbing were not as well established as they are now. As such, it's a divisive venue in terms of boulderers and not universally appreciated by those with an eye for the aesthetic. All is not lost though; it just means a little extra legwork is duly rewarded.

The Rocky Valley area is further from the cafe but still commands a formidable vista over the town and the hills surrounding Wharfedale. Having been largely ignored by early boulderers who understandably preferred the flat grass landings of the standard Ilkley circuit in the pre-bouldering-mat days, Rocky Valley has undergone a surge of development over the last couple of decades. Assuming you've got a pad or two to even out the odd rock-filled landing, there's now plenty on offer, and with scarcely a chipped hold in sight. *Frank* has to be one of the best hard lines from that mid-2000s phase of development. Hard, bunched yet reachy moves lead rightwards across the shield of subtly striated rock, with none of the weird slippy-yet-sharp feeling rock of the main Ilkley circuit. Good toehooking shoes might be worth packing in your bag. Originally given 8a but likely to feel easier if your body size and arm span fits, so the grade given here is an attempt to find the median. A direct finish exists avoiding the right-hand arête, but strangely it's not really significantly more difficult. The 8a+ sit start, however, is.

EARL CRAG

7c Lager Lager Lager (Dave's Groove)

When the classic bouldering film *Stick It* came out in 2001 it was a huge catalyst for the nascent British bouldering scene. Coming just at the start of what would turn out to be a huge boom period, and in the days before ubiquitous online videos, YouTube and streaming, the film was hugely influential. Earl Crag featured in a key segment of the film, depicting a bunch of handy locals and a few Peak raiders out on a cold and frosty winter's day. The delights of Earl had long been appreciated by the Yorkshire scene, but seeing its problems taking centre stage on video really made the rest of the UK – and especially everyone in the Peak – sit up and take notice.

That film scene is still a fairly good showcase of the amazing problems at Earl, and you'd probably not get many people arguing with the fact that *Lager Lager Lager* is top of that particularly well-loaded pile. Only receiving a first ascent in 2000 by Dave Buchanan, its enduring popularity since has cemented its position in the grit bouldering hall of fame. It is not, however, one of those problems where a multitude of ascents somehow breaks the spell. Collective knowledge often leads to problems becoming vastly easier as some sort of magic trick sequence emerges, but not here. This one is still damn hard; surprisingly thin on the feet, powerful, and with a slopey rampline that never really feels as good as you'd like. It pretty much defines the 7c grade on Yorkshire gritstone and remains an essential rite of passage.

Michael Kenyon (left; © Oliver Parkinson), Sam Mawson (centre; © Owen Tomkins), and Rik Battye (right; © Oliver Parkinson) do battle with this frustrating classic.

EARL CRAG

6b The John Dunne Slap

A veritable juggernaut of hard trad and sport in Yorkshire and beyond, John Dunne's contribution to British climbing from the 1980s onwards is formidable. Characterised by numerous first ascents of hard and bold routes, not many of us are capable of following on his heels, so it's fantastic that this problem exists so we can have a John Dunne tick at a manageable grade without risking life and limb.

Sitting on one of the numerous jumbled boulders and buttresses beneath Wainman's Pinnacle at the western end of the crag, *The John Dunne Slap* is one of the many superb problems in the 6s hereabouts. It's grossly unfair to the rest of the crag to single one out as there are just so many brilliant problems before you even get into the crossover highball or solo ones. But it feels appropriate to give a nod to the big man himself. As advertised, it climbs the rib with a big slap, off a pocket-like left-hand slot to a good flatty or, if your legs are too short, via a full dyno. Technicians will also delight in climbing it statically via a poorer right-hand hold, in fact why not do it both ways? You won't have to move the pads very far to find plenty more challenges of interest in the vicinity; the arête just to the left, and the slab left of the arête are both brilliant problems at 6c, *Ron's Arête* and *Ron's Slab* respectively. Nearby, the short *Nice Arête* is another gem, but the truth is that the entire crag is dripping with classics, so get exploring.

Sam Mawson about to 'lay one on' and make the namesake slap.
© Owen Tomkins

YORKSHIRE

SUTTON CLOUGH

7c Treebeard

Opposite Frosty winter conditions put to good use by Oliver Parkinson. © Oliver Parkinson

Earl Crag has so much to offer you'd be forgiven for thinking there couldn't possibly be anything else in the vicinity to compete with it. But hidden away barely a mile from Earl is Mark Katz's modern highball classic. Overlooking a deep shady valley, missing all winter sun completely, it's an atmospheric spot to climb at. Despite only receiving a first ascent in 2013, the various engraved names and dates at the base of the cave-like lower section hint at a much longer history.

While the aspect of *Treebeard* is totally different to its neighbour, the coarse but compact, angular form of the rock is familiar. Steep moves through the roof lead past an ancient chip to decent holds on the lip at the very base of the arête. From here it's long moves on little spaced edges, where anyone with steely fingers well honed at Earl Crag should feel at home. Ideally the moves gaining and then pulling up the arête will be executed as statically as possible to avoid any spectacular dismounts. The landing to the left does drop away abruptly to the valley floor, and that really would be a less than ideal way to end your afternoon.

SHIPLEY GLEN

 Vim

This tall, off-vertical arête just next to the harder *Manson's Wall* is a real local classic. Dating from the 1960s, age has not dulled its potency. It's not to be taken lightly and is still more than capable of putting up a fight even now. Arête climbing interspersed with thin horizontal break holds is something of a gritstone speciality as it doesn't really seem to exist on other rock types as often, not even on sandstone. Yet there are many of these around on grit, and this problem serves as the standard bearer for its brethren up and down the Pennines.

The two problems taking the wall to the left of *Vim*, *Manson's Wall* from a decade later in the crag's development, and *Phil's Wall* a decade later again, both just blast straight up by cranking on thin crimps picked out of the horizontals – another key grit skill to have in your arsenal. Neither are especially highball by modern standards but nevertheless would have required a careful approach back before pads were around. Any volunteers to climb these above a bar towel pinched from a local pub? I suspect not.

At this point a shout-out must be given to all those innumerable routes at Shipley that nudge just beyond the highball into the legit solo. They are for the most part absolutely superb, and accordingly it's a very popular spot for soloing. With the closely bedded grit offering plenty of holds in the numerous horizontal breaks that characterise Shipley, there's an enormous density of usable rock, with almost every square inch of the crag being climbable. Even for the committed boulderer with no real interest in route climbing, an hour spent working through a dozen or so choice lines just inside your comfort zone is an excellent way to spend an afternoon honing your footwork. Building confidence and in general just enjoying moving efficiently on rock – Shipley is more well suited for this than most. Lovely stuff.

Andy Brown treads carefully on this decades-old line. © **Owen Tomkins**

SHIPLEY GLEN

7c+ Red Baron Roof

An unlikely hero of a crag famed more for its short solos and techy walls, *Red Baron* is a great if short-lived classic hanging arête, but the full roof start from underneath really bumps it up into another league. Another Jason Myers problem from 1996, the same year he did *Jason's Roof* at Crookrise. This one is a little easier than the latter, but no less superb.

A true destination problem for the boulderer with aspirations at the high 7s, this ticks a lot of boxes. Easy to work, accessible, plenty of different sequence options to puzzle out, fairly skin friendly by grit standards, and above all a great set of moves. Having said that, it's no pushover. The tensiony moves transferring to heelhooks to gain the final arête demand a little core strength, which often is the first thing to fade when it comes to the final redpoint attempts. Anyone after the quick workmanlike ascent may want to keep some in reserve for their final burns. That said, Shipley is such a great little spot it's not too much of a chore to come back again for another visit.

Right Jon Fullwood makes the transition moves from the horizontal to the vertical. © John Coefield
Left The author on the old-school *Manson's Wall*. © John Coefield

GRIT BLOCS

BELL BANK WOOD

7c Gritty Shaker

Under a mile from the centre of Bingley, and within a busy country park, Bell Bank Wood in the St Ives estate seems an unlikely home to a true off-the-beaten-track hidden gem. The estate actually sports a number of recently discovered problems dotted around, but *Gritty Shaker* is the clear standout line which would be a showstopper at any grit crag. Ease of access makes it good to combine with a visit elsewhere, although this is contingent upon actually successfully climbing it. From a sit start it goes at 8a, but most will find the standing jump-start method more than enough sport.

The hillside here barely offers any horizontal ground at all, and when coupled with the geometry of the double-curved arête it's a little bewildering to comprehend at first, as depending on where you stand it looks either slabby or overhanging, or both at the same time. The tall holdless wall to the left of the arête bears fine horizontal striations hinting at its local cousin Shipley Glen, but in contrast to that crag's flat landings and superb wall climbing *Gritty Shaker* is balancey, powerful and, due to the slope of the ground, instantly exposed feeling. The inevitable barn-door seems to be poised to fling you down the slope at any moment.

With no face holds to come to the rescue and no fortuitously placed crimps, keeping physics at bay for just long enough to climb it is all about body position. But unlike a lot of technical grit arêtes, don't expect to just balance your way up this, as it still requires some oompf. Even the initial jump start can quickly become draining after several attempts, and you will need plenty in the tank for turning the second bulge, after which an easing off of difficulties comes just in time for the high top-out.

John Coefield engages 'try quite hard' mode.

GRIT BLOCS

CLATTERING STONES

7a **Androsterone**

The makings of a classic cold sunny winter session at Clattering Stones: Matt Thompson and Rob Smith sampling the delights of *Mantilimar*, *Androsterone*, *Morning Sickness* and *Linea Negra* (clockwise from top).

The crags and outcrops clustered around Widdop Reservoir enjoy an odd combination of feeling remote, yet accessible; they are wild yet the human influence is everywhere. Only a few hundred metres from the road as the crow flies (and from the Lancashire border!), nevertheless expect to spend a bit of effort getting up here. Luckily most of the landings are decent, and the problems of average stature, so huge quantities of padding aren't required. The Clattering Stones are remarkably free of scrittle, offering good solid rock with brilliant views on fair days and catching the early sun. Still, expect to get cold if there's a strong northerly.

The Clatterjack block sports a long wall of solid shady grit, just off vertical and the perfect height for bouldering. Each line on this wall competes keenly with anything else of the given grade and style. *Androsterone*, like most of the problems here, follows a pregnancy-themed naming tradition, and is probably the pick of the bunch. But, in reality, it would be hard to leave here having not sampled any of the other obvious challenges. *Linea Negra* in particular is a deceptively tricky little number.

Not far away is the large boulder with an open groove taken by *Morning Sickness*, a rarity in being a good mid-grade dyno that's genuinely easiest as an actual dyno, although the static method is still a great sequence.

WIDDOP

 Fight on Black

We talk a lot about what makes grit special – the friction, the slopey mantel top-outs, the supremacy of technique. But if there's a dark art of grit that divides opinion like no other then it's pebble pulling.

Pebbles are not a phenomenon unique to gritstone, as they can be found in other types of sedimentary rock (see the Churnet Valley for what happens when pebbles multiply and take over entire crags). But no other rock types seem to be as prone to pebbles forming a sparse but crucial aspect of many climbs. These tiny nuggets of solid quartz, already having led an interesting life in some river or other millions of years ago, can easily end up being as famous as the routes and problems themselves – see the famous *Beau Geste* pebble at Froggatt (or what's left of it), or ones where the entire problem revolves around them, like Almscliff's *Pebble Wall*.

Having to use the odd pebble on a grit slab is one thing, but actually having to pull hard on one on a steeper line is a different ball game. Opinions differ on the best way to hold any given pebble. Some will crimp over a pebble, stacking fingers; this gives the good grip but also has the highest chance of instantly tearing a fingertip pad open. Some will pinch a pebble between the index finger and thumb, as if turning a tiny volume knob on a stereo; mechanically strong but with little flesh to soften the pain. Others will just hook a finger over and try not to think about it too much. But whatever your preferred method, expect it to hurt. The best option, as always, is to not need too many attempts.

With that in mind, *Fight on Black* will take a little gritting of the teeth to see this one safely in the bag. The upper slopey break is exactly as unhelpful as it looks, but to even get that far you must first master the huge sharp white pebble for the left hand. It's a horrid hold, but an inescapably brilliant solution.

Marco Giudice (top) and Adam Long (right) make the most of the fading dusk light on *Fight on Black*. Nearby *Pickpocket's Wall* (above; climber Andy Emery) is a stern test of the fingers.

GORPLE

8a Chabal

Some problems shout loudly. Big roofs, soaring arêtes, blank slabs – you know the type. Standout bangers you can recognise a mile away. But not everything on gritstone shouts loudly, not everything brilliant announces its presence like your mate's gobby friend arriving at the pub wearing brand new trainers. *Chabal* is no *Careless Torque*, no *Superbloc*, no *Lanny Bassham*, but bear with me here.

Mark Katz's modern classic is one of those problems which, on the surface, ticks none of the boxes. Not really a blindingly compelling line, no obvious moves, no obvious solution, and slightly scrittley rock. A wild location, but domesticated by the presence of the shooting hut. Yet it somehow manages to condense all the gritstone weirdness you could ever want, but didn't realise you needed, into one problem. From the fingery pull off the deck from sitting prepare for battle with crimps, slopers, undercuts, kneebars, heelhooks and a little scrittle. Cool conditions and a breeze are a prerequisite; even winter sun can quickly make the friction head south. Good luck trying to train specifically for this, as nothing will help except just doing a lot of everything.

The only thing missing really is a humiliating slopey mantel finish, as thankfully our blushes are saved by a relatively amenable top-out. There are a number of other worthwhile problems at Gorple, some tasty mid-grade walls and bulges, although if truth be told, if 8a-ish is your grade then *Chabal* will suck you in for the full session. Just make sure you bring a warm jacket for when the sun finally drops behind the hillside opposite, and save a little in the tank for that one last attempt as the conditions skyrocket.

Rob Smith, wisely equipped with a full set of kneepads, gets stuck in on this deceptively steep masterpiece.

SCOUT HUT

6c Needle of Dreams

As the road to Widdop winds its way up from Hebden Bridge, tucked away off one hairpin bend lies this little crag, almost hidden from view. Well, 'little' in terms of reputation and status, not being one of the area's 'big' famous crags. But arriving beneath the looming pale bulk of the main buttress it's not hard to feel very small indeed.

Remarkably, the outstanding highball *Needle of Dreams* had to wait until 1996 for a first ascent, but this still predates widespread use of bouldering mats. Originally requiring a pure soloing mentality: either do it, or if you can't make the long locks be sure you can downclimb. These days the largely flat landings allow this line, or the neighbouring 7a *Strone Road*, to be enjoyed – and even fallen off – fairly safely, if you have a half-decent pad stack and vigilant spotters. Even one or two mats should at least take the sting out of bottling the top move and dropping in control.

Although it has to be said it helps enormously to be operating inside your grade comfort zone. If 6c is your absolute limit then the extended top moves on big rough slopers on *Needle of Dreams* could easily turn into a harrowing experience, especially in warm conditions.

Scout Hut is something of a sheltered afternoon suntrap, though this does make it valuable in the cooler months as an option if things turn grim 'up high' on the moorland crags. You'll be buzzing at the top though, whatever your level. Bring a confident head, some pads and enjoy – and don't forget a camera!

Above Andy Emery makes the crucial long lock to better holds on *Needle of Dreams*.   **Left** Jason Pickles sets up for the crux of *Strone Road*.

GRIT BLOCS

MYTHOLM EDGE

7b+ Tony's Wall

Rough holds hidden in the woods – Andy Emery (above) and Marco Giudice (opposite) investing a bit of skin into *Tony's Wall*.

Sometimes perceptions of quality are as much to do with managing expectations as they are with quantifiable variables. Things that don't look great at first but are unexpectedly pleasant can often feel more rewarding than something which looks amazing but disappoints upon getting acquainted. Mytholm is a classic example of a venue where hopes are not high upon parking up next to a tottering quarry full of chossy-looking rock. No disrespect intended to fans of Mytholm Quarry – yes there *is* climbing in it – but for the bouldering connoisseur the main event is elsewhere.

In all honesty, the just-about-freestanding block of *Tony's Wall* doesn't seem that promising upon initial inspection. Dark, hidden away, not prone to catching much breeze to help the conditions, and a cap of grass and moss which keeps dampness lingering. The holds are obvious, maybe it's just basic pulling? But once engaged in battle with the frustrating slopey blobs, grinding skin on the roughly textured holds, getting the body position just right, the deceptively steep wall draws you in, and will win you round.

JUMBLE HOLE CLOUGH

7c Red Rooster

This steep clough cut into the side of the Calder Valley between Hebden Bridge and Todmorden is better known to climbers as the home of The Roost, a huge steep quarried face, unfortunately now off limits for climbing. But the valley, which is part of the traditional boundary between Yorkshire and Lancashire, still has a little something up its sleeve for the boulderer.

Perched right up at the top end of the clough on the Yorkshire side, overlooking the impressive ruins of Staups Mill, there are some natural outcrops with recently developed bouldering. Facing south, it's an idyllic spot to catch a little sun through the trees and get to grips with some rough slopers to the sound of the rushing river. Dave Sutcliffe's *Red Rooster* is the standout line and takes the obvious big prow from the right-hand side, following a good rail until the arête falls to hand, heelhooks are engaged, and the final tantalising few moves are unlocked.

Grit season doesn't have to end in March – the author making use of the cool shade in late spring amid the bluebells.

YORKSHIRE

LANCASHIRE

GRIT BLOCS

THORN CRAG

 Ouzel Thorn

The author enjoying this unsung gem in balmy T-shirt weather on New Year's Day.

Undoubtedly the jewel in Lancashire's gritstone crown, Thorn Crag perches on the edge of Tarnbrook Fell like ramparts, with the scattering of silvery grey boulders contrasting against the brown fellside, with an enviable view out to the Irish Sea.

Thorn feels a long way from everywhere else in the gritstone universe, but the recognisable DNA of moorland gritstone is still present. The obligatory long walk-in is rewarded with unique shapes and strong lines on superbly fine-grained gritstone. In fact, on the less-well-travelled problems you're more likely to feel a slight sandiness under the fingers which is more reminiscent of the high fell Northumberland sandstone than the usual coarse gritstone scrittle.

Ouzel Thorn lies well up on the hillside above most of the other bouldering, taking the right-hand arête of the fine square slab with the aid of a crack. All pretty straightforward until the crack runs out, making the committing crux on smears occur right at the top. Thankfully a good flat landing helps make this unsung gem a memorable experience for all the right reasons.

Just down the hill is the Diamond boulder, with some more immaculate smearing slab problems to contend with, heels low, with complete focus. *Private Press* in particular is as pure a smearing exercise as you'll find on grit. If you fancy yourself as a slab magician, try the unclimbed line left of *Ouzel Thorn* – a single shallow pocket marks the way. If you can get your foot in this somehow, you're golden.

THORN CRAG

7b+ Bad Moon Rising

Notching things up a gear from the superb slab lines, *Bad Moon Rising* is arguably the essential steep modern-style problem at Thorn at this grade. First climbed by Neil 'Nige' Kershaw in 2003, this chunky overhanging arête sits on its own below the main crag. Commanding a formidable view out across the shooting track and the Trough of Bowland beyond, it's understandably popular. Expect heelhooking, beautifully textured slopers and a bit of physicality.

Uphill from the *Bad Moon* boulder, past the next tier of great easier problems, up on Thorn Crag proper, lies the off-vertical wall of *Return of The Fly*. This 7c+ could have been parachuted in direct from Crookrise. A blind crack traces a line up the wall before running out unhelpfully, where smears and poor pockets lead to a better high pocket, leaving just a careful top out. Even if this isn't your bag, it's worth the walk up just to eyeball John Gaskins' other main contribution to Thorn, the almost-mythical slopey bulging arête line which dominates the crag: *A Moment of Clarity*. Wow etc.

Right Kitty Morrison makes the crux move to a beautiful handful of finest Bowland grit. © Sam Lawson

LANCASHIRE

GRIT BLOCS

THORN CRAG

7a+ Mothership Reconnection

The boulders over on the western side of the main track snaking up to the fell-top plateau at Thorn sport a formidable concentration of problems, complete with plenty of interesting rock shapes and formations, all boasting the best view out towards Morecambe Bay. The 6c traverse of *Elemental*, a fine iron rail sweeping fortuitously along the lip of a boulder, gives one of the most compelling traverse lines at the grade anywhere. But don't let this cluster of boulders completely sidetrack you – save a little energy for *Mothership Reconnection*.

Nestled in the heart of a huge jumble of blocks, the compact slopey prow sports a perfectly flat rock platform landing to rival any man-made patio. The right-hand side of the prow is part of a huge ramp feature, providing ample slopey handfuls of sugar-textured grit; meanwhile, the subtly undulating left-hand side gives just enough distinct holds for the other hand. It is, it must be admitted, a short problem, but the low start on opposing sidepulls goes some of the way towards making sure it doesn't feel over too soon.

For a crag that feels so far from the rest of Pennine grit, the presence of a brand-new-looking shooting lodge and very well-maintained vehicle tracks snaking around the crag do give a slightly domestic mood to the fellside which perhaps takes the edge off the remote feeling of Thorn. However, for a truly wild experience, those with a pad and a good set of legs on them might do well to check out Wolfhole Crag. One of the most remote grit bouldering spots around, being a further half an hour or so from Thorn, it's reputedly the stuff legends are made of.

LANCASHIRE

Order among the chaos – the author on *Mothership Reconnection*.

WILTON 3

6a The Square

The legacy of the North's industrial heritage is felt all across the Pennines. It's in the culture, in the language, in the buildings and in the social order that persists today. In climbing terms, it's most obviously felt by the prevalence of quarrying. In many places, like the Wilton quarries, the rock was used to literally build the industrial towns and cities hereabouts. But since that violent beginning of rock being unceremoniously torn from the ground, nature inevitably returns to soften the raw edges a little, to reclaim some territory, and people themselves repurpose these scars on the moorland for other uses.

At Wilton we have the strange spectacle of climbers sharing the quarry with the local shooting club. It's an unusual symbiosis, but seems to work. I can't comment on the quality of the shooting, but it's fair to say the bouldering in these quarries is something of an acquired taste, valued more highly by the local than the visitor. But valued it is, and maybe the rest of us shouldn't be so quick to dismiss the delights of these quarries. Certainly, there are compelling lines to be climbed amid impressive rock architecture, crimps to be crimped, smears to be trusted, and a unique ambience. On problems like *The Square*, catching the morning light on a late autumn day, it's easy to get lost in the movement for a few moments.

LANCASHIRE

Lancs quarries in their best light – Matt Thompson on *The Square*, and its left-hand variant, in midwinter morning sunshine.

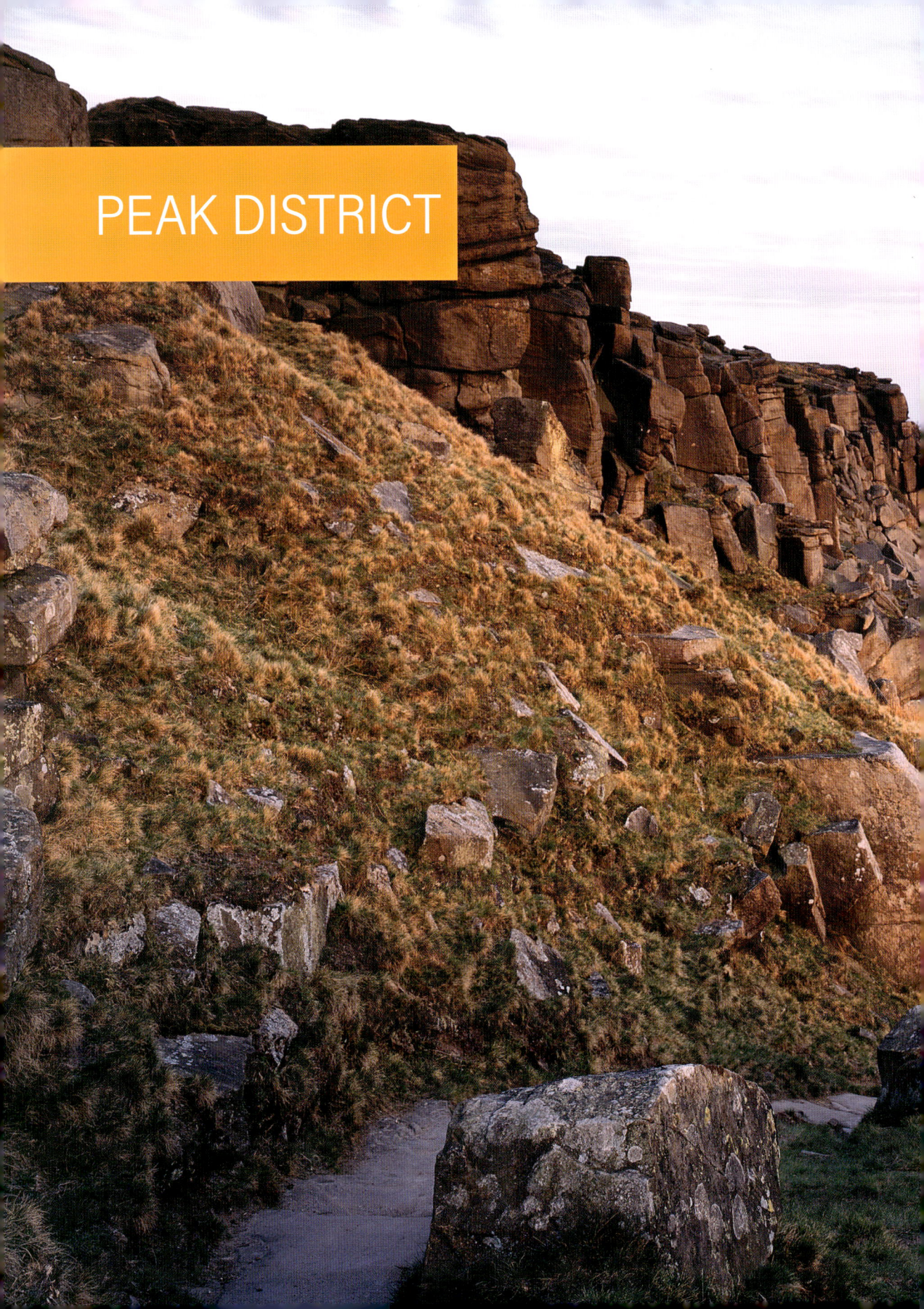

PEAK DISTRICT

WEST NAB

7a Archery

At the very northern tip of the Peak, West Nab sits at a lofty 500 metres above sea level. Although it's not the most northern crag within the Peak District National Park – that trophy goes to nearby Shooter's Nab – this jumble of gritstone atop a hill does stake an oft-repeated claim to being the highest point in West Yorkshire. A rather confusing claim, as it turns out, since the summit of nearby Black Hill is a good eighty-five metres higher and also within the county. Hopefully this piece of trivia will win one of you a pub quiz one day.

Tedious topographical details aside, it's a cracking place to visit. As you'd imagine, the crag gets all the weather conditions the Pennines can throw at it. Brutal in cold, windy weather, yet a superb place to drink in the expansive view on a sunny day. Throughout, the rock quality is up there with the best – not much of the famed moorland gritstone scrittle to be found.

The circuit of friendly sized low-to-mid-grade problems is enough of a draw in itself, but tucked away on the north-eastern flank of the crag, enjoying some welcome shelter from the westerlies, is West Nab's 'king line'. *Archery* is an arête in the finest grit tradition: technical, good landing, and tall enough that the feeling of the top hold in your hand is a welcome one. It's no giveaway, but for something more challenging don't miss the fabled *Access Denied* 7c+ traverse, by far the hardest thing here but a worthy grind on slopers nonetheless.

Matt Thompson shows the way on this Kirklees classic.

WIMBERRY

7b Fish Arête Sit-Start

While the Chew Valley sometimes feels a little isolated from the rest of the Peak District gritstone, that does mean it has its own inimitable charms. The entire area is big on character, and Wimberry is a crag with more character than most.

Strong lines, dark walls, north facing, overlooking a boulder field, and plenty of hard frightening routes: Wimberry crag bears some similarity to Burbage South. A Burbage South with everything dialled up to 11. The boulder field is a little like this too. Everything is bigger and a little fiercer than its eastern cousin. The problems are bigger, generally harder, and Burbage's bullet-hole scars are replaced with chipped holds. Sadly, this has meant that the current generation is robbed of many of the possible incredible lines on offer. Having said that, the further you walk from the car park, the fewer and further between the chips become. It seems chisel enthusiasts are fundamentally quite lazy, to our great relief.

Of the untainted classics the Wimberry boulders host, a few stand out as truly top class. The highball slab of *Winsome* is an unmissable 7a+ when clean, and one requiring a cool head and ideally a couple of pads. *Miles' Slab* lacks the height aspect, but more than makes up for that with a frustrating and difficult sequence. Looks easy, and it would be if the scoop in the slab was big enough to mantel into. But the pick of the bunch is surely *Fish Arête Sit-Start*. Powerful compression moves on impeccable rock, a perfect landing and, for a relatively short problem, it's actually fairly sustained, droppable right to the end. A great problem to finish a spring evening on with the sitting sun catching the arête – marvellous.

A hard-earned Chew classic on impeccable rough gritstone. Jon Fullwood (opposite) and Steve Delderfield (below; © **Mike Delderfield**).

WHARNCLIFFE

7c Cazu Marzu

I'm going to come clean – Wharncliffe isn't technically gritstone, not by the strictest geological definition. However, the sprawling one-and-a-half-mile edge line of dark angular rock makes a good claim to being the birthplace of British outcrop climbing in the 1880s and is entirely gritstone in spirit, so it gets the nod for this book. The crag's many buttresses and boulders keep throwing up quality problems to this day, with no sign of slowing down. That's quite some longevity.

A pivotal figure in Wharncliffe's development as a modern bouldering venue is Jon Fullwood, so it's only right we highlight one of Jon's best recent additions here. Nestled away in the woods at the southern end of the edge line, when you search out this one you're much more likely to bump into dog walkers or mountain bikers than other climbers. *Cazu Marzu* stays true to the Wharncliffe trad-route archetype, being stiff basic pulls between angular holds. There's nowhere to hide if your finger strength isn't up to scratch, although neighbouring lines of the arête and the brilliantly named *The 87 Bus* (because it goes from Lowedges to High Green) offer worthwhile consolation prizes. Nearby, the unique Swiss-style 8a tilted wall of *Kobe*, courtesy of Ned Feehally, is the jewel in Wharncliffe's crown for those with a wide enough wingspan.

A taste of the modern circuit – Adam Long on *The 87 Bus* (top), John Coefield on *Grüne Hölle* (left) and *Cazu Marzu* (opposite).

GRINAH STONES

7-ish Unnamed arête

There's a danger when discussing Grinah Stones that it could be oversold as a sort of magical, almost mythical, venue. Pristine pocketed slabs, towering obelisks, steep walls, all of fine-grained and remarkably scrittle-free moorland gritstone that most of the other crags on Kinder or Bleaklow would kill to be made of. The commitment made in setting off up there means you're probably not going to make the journey unless there's a good forecast, giving the illusion that Grinah occupies some sort of Californian microclimate where the sun always shines, the sky is always cobalt-blue, the breeze is always keen, and the midges are non-existent.

With this in mind, in the interest of not leaving anyone disappointed, some negativity is required. To access one of the highest elevation grit bouldering venues in the country, and certainly in this book, you're looking at least two and a half miles of uphill trudge via the shortest approach. You may get lost on the way. There is no convenient place to hang your portable fingerboard from. The problems are often high, committing and in need of a brush, with no tell-tale chalk to unlock sequences. You won't have the time to fully discover everything, and there is no guidebook or topo to shortcut the exploration. You will probably be exhausted by the approach, and yet you will still not have carried enough water with you. If you turn your ankle dropping off a highball it's one hell of a long crawl back to the road. And what's worse, there is deliberately no recorded information on names, grades or first ascents of anything, so you won't even have any bragging rights, logbook ticks or monetizable social media kudos.

You'll definitely hate this tall slender arête with an insecure crux at the very top, with a sprung landing of bilberry bushes to rest your pads upon. It definitely won't be the most satisfying ascent you make during the most memorable day out you'll have all year. Take my advice: play it safe, don't go.

Simon Wilson (top), Jon Fullwood (bottom) and Adam Long (opposite) wishing they'd not bothered.

HOWSHAW TOR

7c+ Panopticon

It's hard to believe that, until 2013, one of the standout problems on the entirety of Pennine gritstone lay unclimbed, unseen, yet comfortably within Sheffield's borders. *Panopticon* lives up to its name by giving the impression you can see pretty much everywhere from the problem, although you can't see it from anywhere. And part of its charm is the feeling of remoteness, despite the fact you can be back at the road in a little over thirty minutes.

But that's only part of the appeal. It's the perfect height, impeccable rock quality, sports a good landing, and has powerful, fingery, yet physical moves. Remote yet accessible; complex yet solvable. The double toehooking feet-first method for turning the lip gives a truly memorable finish that really puts *Panopticon* up there with the best of the best. If this doesn't put a smile on your face, then you'd better check for a heartbeat – although it has to be said the taller climber will have an easier time of it.

Fish Finger Kid on the same roof is almost as good and shares the same finish – well worth doing. The rest of the crag offers a great circuit in the 6b to 7b range: generally clean and compact rock, cool in summer, and largely free from the typical moorland scrittle. Those who find *Panopticon* a little easy are well catered for with lines like *Broke Beak Mountain*, 7c+, *Bloodhound*, 8a, and the 8a traverse line of *Hare Today Gone Tomorrow* – the latter almost being a sort of gritstone *Slashface* for the moorland Fred Nicoles out there.

John Coefeld getting stuck into *Sneakin' the Beak In* – the standing start of *Broke Beak Mountain* (above) and *Panopticon* (opposite).

DOVESTONE TOR

5+ Perfect Porthole Problem

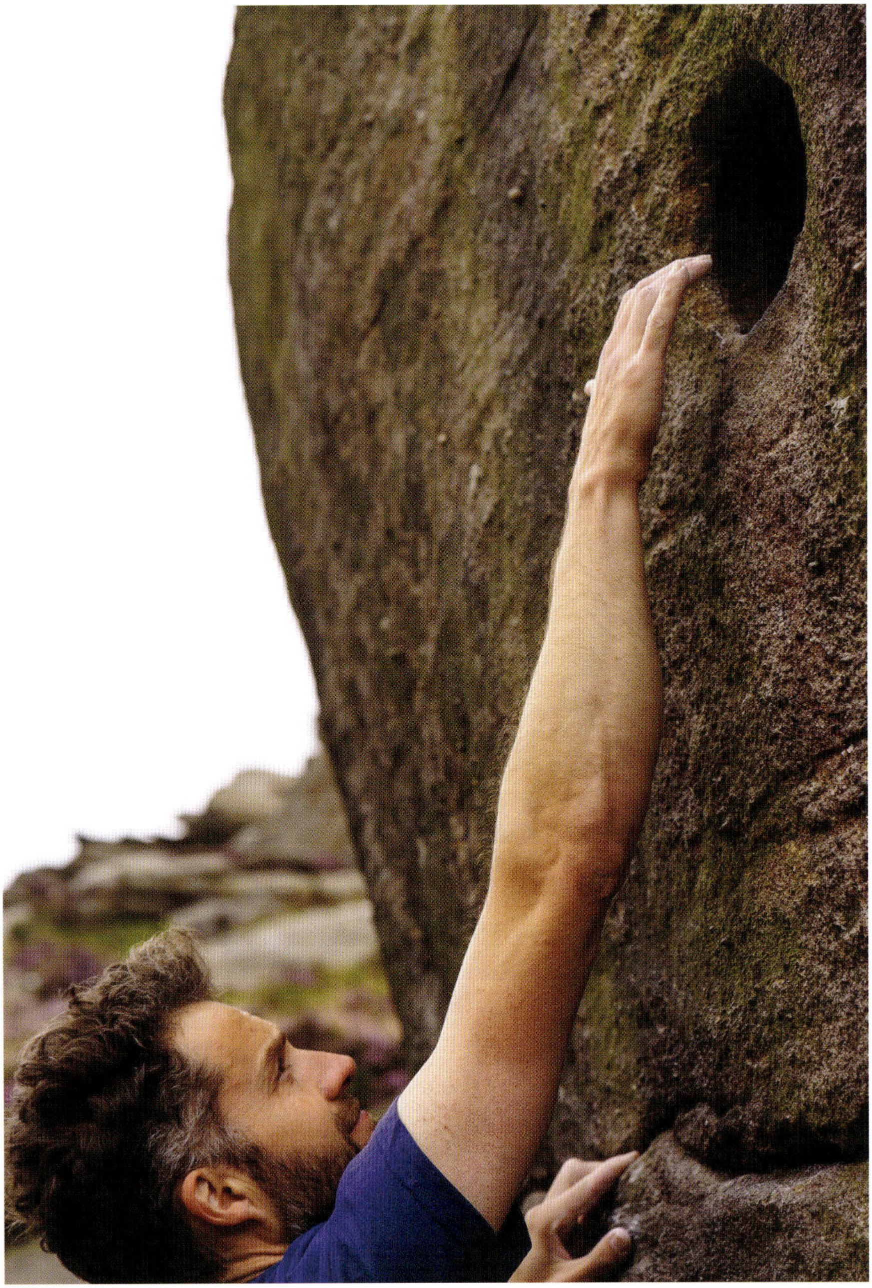

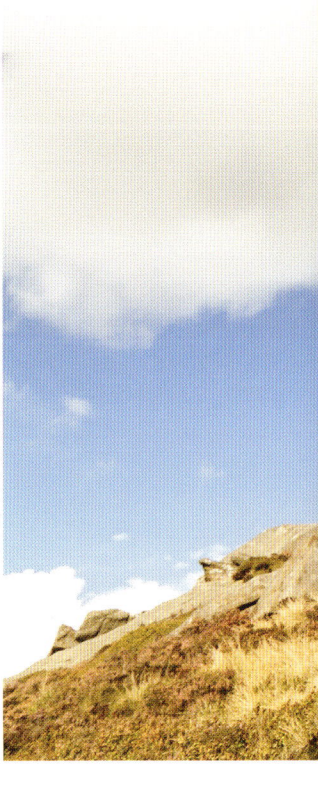

The aforementioned circular 'Hueco' pocket is remarkable in itself, but this problem's biggest selling point is actually that it provides a decent excuse to make the trip up on to Derwent Edge to explore the bouldering available on the numerous tors and outcrops around here. At its best on a breezy late summer day when the heather is flowering; like its near neighbour Howshaw, Derwent can provide a welcome escape from the heat. Most of the bouldering is at the mid to lower grades too, which also helps prevent too much of an ego bruising in warmer weather.

Rock quality can vary but the best things are on top-quality moorland gritstone, so saddle up, make the walk up, and explore. Numerous walls, arêtes and roof problems exist on Dovestone Tor, but there's also plenty to check out on the other crags hereabouts, including the prominent Coach and Horses, and Back Tor. Those with a confident head might enjoy the Hurkling Stones which sport a potentially highballable E6 6c route, *Sick Arête*. The landing is good, and the walk from the A57 isn't all that far. Get stuck in.

A remarkable lower-grade gem, definitely worth the walk. John Coefield (opposite; © **Adam Long**) and Jon Barton (above; © **John Coefield**).

GRIT BLOCS

RIVELIN

7c+ Master Kush

John Coefield on *Acid Reign* (above) in complete contrast of style to *Master Kush* (opposite).

In contrast to its near neighbours on the Eastern Edges, Rivelin offers a completely different ambience. Relatively sheltered from the wind, catching what little winter sun there is, and rarely busy, the crag remains a perennial favourite of Sheffield climbers during the harsh winter months.

On *Master Kush* in particular, the contrast offered from the standard grit experience is made clear. Brutally steep and cruxy; the usual considerations of gritstone finesse and technique give way to a simple requirement for raw power and plenty of it. Regular users of steep plywood boards will love this one.

Luckily, it's not all so in-your-face – the crag sports a fantastic highball circuit through the grades on excellent rock, with *Acid Reign* being the obvious eye-pleaser. Moving leftwards into the deeply cut, quarried bays, the modern classics of *Happy Campus* and *Cheeks 'n' Beaks* await among the esoterica.

GRIT BLOCS

BAMFORD

7b Spike

Some gritstone crags seem timeless, like nothing ever changes and never will. At others, progress is marked more obviously; time definitely doesn't stand still at Bamford.

As you top out a problem and accidentally photobomb a surprised Instagrammer getting obligatory selfies with the Ashopton Viaduct in the background, you may well consider the curious feedback loop of social media – the algorithm effect – which leads to certain places becoming unusually popular. Or you might glance down from the crag and be reminded of the villages in the valley which were demolished and flooded in the early 1940s to create Ladybower Reservoir. Did you know there's a two-metre-high tunnel running right under Bamford Edge, then under Stanage, taking water from Ladybower into Rivelin Dams? Well, you do now.

Bouldering at Bamford has progressed enormously over the last couple of decades, from being virtually non-existent, to a full and varied circuit. Key to this was a piece of legislation, the Countryside and Rights of Way Act 2000, which gave more or less free access to a crag which had historically suffered from severely restricted access due to grouse shooting. The BMC's 1989 *Stanage* guide instructs climbers to phone the game keeper to ask for permission to visit. Without the CRoW Act, Bamford would likely still be very much a backwater for both boulderers and social media influencers.

Jon Fullwood has been one of the main catalysts for change on the Bamford bouldering circuit, putting the hours in to search out new lines, clear landings, clean, climb and document new problems, particularly at the far northern end of the crag. His 'king line' here remains *Spike* from 2009, named after his son. It's no pushover at the grade, and is a worthy companion line to Ron Fawcett's classic E6 *Jasmine* (named after Ron's daughter), just to the right. Just to the left, Sam Lawson's 8a *Captain Birdseye* also looks destined to be a minor classic for those in the know, although it's going to make an odd name for a child.

Ned Feehally on the picturesque Bamford circuit – *Flaky Fluster* (above) and *Spike* (right).

STANAGE

Solomon Grundy

Plumb-vertical 8a walls are something of a rarity on gritstone. Arêtes, slabs and bulges are in good supply, but somehow walls are thinner on the ground – if you pardon the pun. A solution to an apparently blank wall is something really special. Nowhere is the breach of the apparently impossible so obvious, after all everyone can identify and relate to the vertical.

The constructed urban world offers no shortage of verticals, but in climbing terms something about the geometry of the vertical means the margins for finding the perfect hard wall of natural gritstone are infinitesimally narrow. Only one or two variables separate the impossible and disappointingly trivial, not least at Stanage, where the geology of the crag favours break-to-break climbing. Such a premium-quality compact wall at the magical 8a grade of just the right height, and sporting a decent landing, is a rare find indeed.

Far from the crowds, Ned Feehally (top) and Char Williams (bottom right) on *Solomon Grundy*, and Frances Bensley on the nearby hidden *Soft Top Beetle* (bottom left).

PEAK DISTRICT

STANAGE

 **D.I.Y.**

Iconic winter gritstone dialled all the way up to eleven: Toby Wilson on *D.I.Y.* (opposite) and Tom Peckitt landing *Deliverance* (above).

The famed free-standing boulders of Stanage Plantation and the Crescent Arête area hardly need any introduction. Many iconic classics abound, but it can't be ignored that popularity exacts a heavy toll on some of these problems, especially since much of the rock on the boulders is not quite bullet-hard. Polish is one thing, but hold erosion is a much more serious problem, exacerbated by an undeserved reputation for being fast drying after rain. Even the seemingly invincible Crescent Arête boulder suffers from a deteriorating landing and excessive wear to the ledge at the base of the arête.

What Stanage does have, however, is several miles of crag to explore. Relatively unscathed problems can still be enjoyed away from the crowds, especially for those willing to go a little further from the car, and maybe a little higher above a pad. Numerous highball classics dot the crag along the section from the Causeway to the Popular End – *Shirley's Shining Temple, Daydreamer, Shock Horror Slab, Silk, Satin, Back in the YMCA, Nightsalt, Central Buttress Direct, Four Star*; the list goes on. A favourite among these is Graham Hoey's 1981 addition *D.I.Y.*; technical and airy moves to enter a slight groove which thankfully eases off at just the right moment. Catch it on a winter's afternoon when the light, the friction and the enjoyment are all off the scale. BOOM.

STANAGE

8a Careless Torque

There's no two ways about it, *Careless Torque* is the jewel in Stanage's bouldering crown, if not the entire Peak. If not the country, if we're honest. Dripping with history, replete with superlatives and the purest line imaginable: the arête swoops down gracefully some six or seven metres from the apex of the boulder and tantalisingly ends only just within reach of the floor. First climbed by Ron Fawcett, arguably the greatest British climber of his generation, a good ten years or so before bouldering pads were available. Just think about that for a second.

Even today with thick pads, modern shoes, beta videos and all the advances in climbing training over the last thirty-odd years, it actually receives fewer ascents than you might imagine. Thankfully the bar to entry is so high – both physically and metaphorically – it is spared the endless traffic which more accessible Stanage classics suffer from. It remains beyond the grasp of most of us, but it's always good to have a dream.

Malcolm Smith on his early repeat (right; © **Ray Wood**), while a more recent 'pad party' sees Dan Varian reach the top (left; © **Adam Long**).

STANAGE

3+ The High Road

Above A gritstone expedition in miniature: William Parry treads carefully on the upper arête of *The High Road*.
Opposite Naomi Abboud enjoys one of the many traverses hereabouts and Julia Mariella maintains focus on the undercutting start of *The High Road*.

Don't let the modest grade fool you, this easily overlooked gem tiptoeing across the lip of a huge slab is a truly great mini expedition, especially memorable for those in the early stages of their bouldering career. The landing slopes away, and the nature of standing up into the undercut flake means the feeling of exposure is instant. For those only used to climbing indoors on distinct holds this can be a bit of an education, but what better place is there to learn? A cool head and a confident approach soon see you at the final slabby arête, where you emerge from that bubble of concentration and enjoy blasting up to the summit.

Around the short walls, slabs and bulges in the vicinity, it's possible to piece together a great little varied circuit of low-to-mid-grade problems of a high standard on great rock. No big names, nothing too shouty, but brilliant nevertheless. Best enjoyed on a late summer evening when the steady stream of dogwalkers has thinned to a trickle and it's just you, the breeze and the lengthening shadows.

BURBAGE WEST

7b+ West Side Story

One of John Allen's finest contributions to the gritstone canon. Char Williams (above) and Ben Bransby (opposite; © **Adam Long**).

A problem that needs no introduction, which renders the rest of this page of text superfluous. I am contractually obligated to write something though, so let's reflect a little on what makes this a special problem.

Firstly, the line itself is enticing, slap bang up the middle of a clean wall. This is pure bouldering. Not seeking the line of least resistance of the easier arête or the path around the back, instead we let the rock show us where the most aesthetic solution is. Slightly tarnished by the possibilities of lesser variations to each side, the central line draws you in and is strong enough to maintain its integrity. From the moment you pull on you know where you're aiming, and it's straight up the wall to the top.

Secondly, the climbing. There's a sequence for everyone on this, every height catered for, with more holds than any one sequence actually requires, so it's just a matter of searching out the right one for you. Despite seeming vertical it is actually overhanging by a few degrees, a fact which will be of some comfort to those who find it unexpectedly difficult. It's undeniably frustrating – any given foothold can pop if not fully weighted, and the margin between each handhold feeling terrible or brilliant is narrow, separated only by conditions and body position microbeta. Even once you've already done it, even having it 'wired', it's never a pushover. Always ready to spit you off if you drop your guard, but when it all works, when the friction is high and you execute it perfectly, there's nothing better. Like you're just levitating up the wall with no effort expended. Concentrating on staying relaxed, the solution to the perfect gritstone conundrum.

Finally, there's the history. First climbed in 1985 by gritstone legend John Allen, who famously almost did it in his first session. An early example of the famed English 7a grade, it was always set to be sought after, popularity assured, and that's proved to be very much the case. It's also worth considering that the landing originally will have been about a foot higher than it is now, and flat grass. The rock itself, being absolutely premium-quality grit, has actually stood up to the traffic remarkably well, but it's the landing that's taken the brunt of the punishment. It remains to be seen what the solution to the ground erosion issue is in the longer term. But at least everyone carrying huge pads now means one thing: there's no excuse for bailing at the break and not topping out.

BURBAGE NORTH

6a+ All Quiet on the Eastern Front

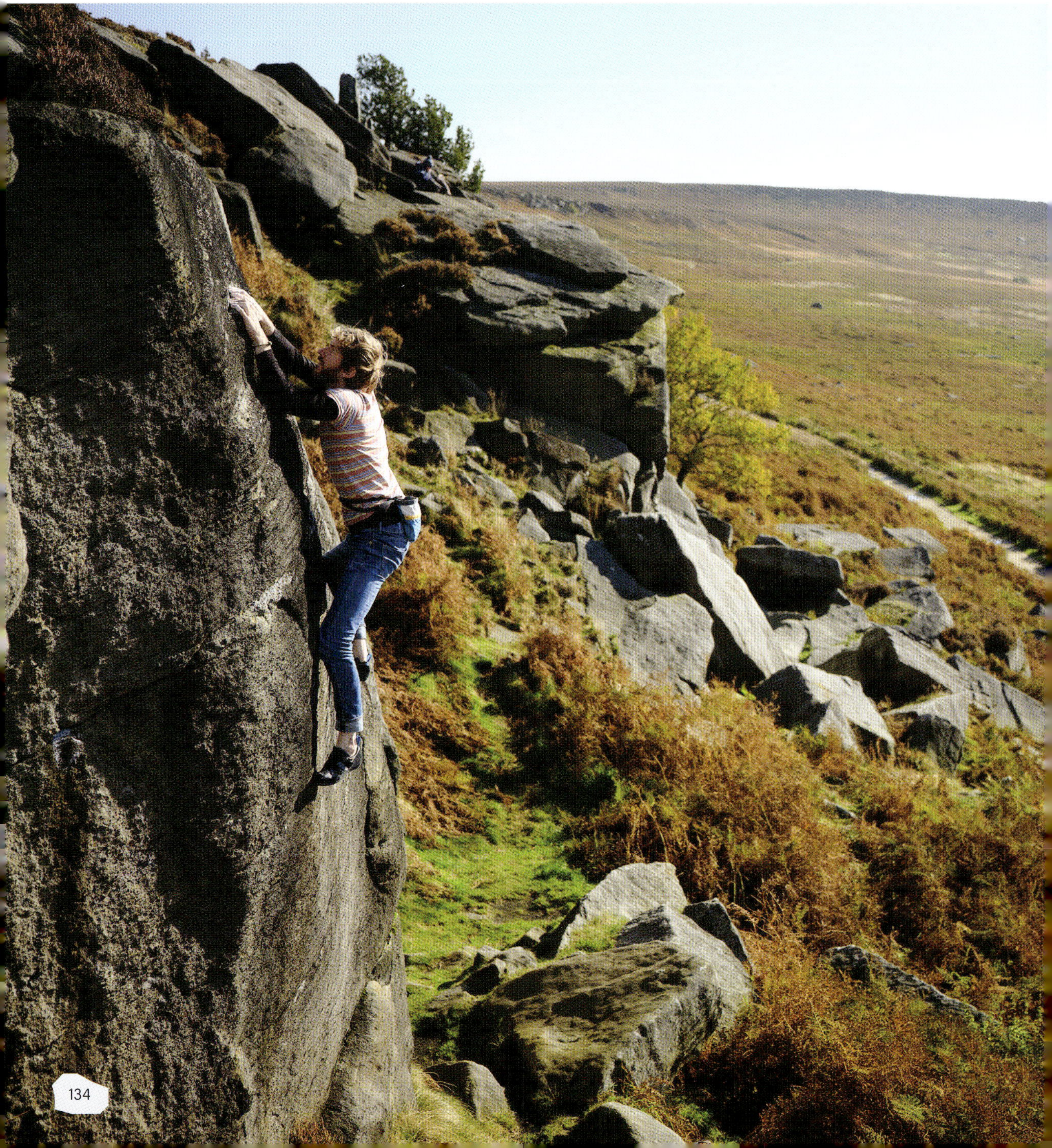

Burbage is one of the quintessential Sheffield after-work crags. One of the first places you'll reach travelling westward out of town, it's quick drying, fairly sheltered, and the bouldering starts only a few metres from the car. So it's a great place for anyone under time pressure, and the crag really comes into its own in spring when the days are just starting to feel a little longer. Just what the doctor ordered when you *really* need some time on dry rock after yet another long, damp and miserable winter. The first session where you make it out to Burbage for the last half an hour of daylight feels like an utter joy. Dry rock! Daylight! It's no wonder Burbage is a perennial favourite of the Sheffield cognoscenti.

A week later and you are blessed with an extra twelve minutes of light, the feel for the grit returning after too much time on plastic. You might work your way further through the standard Burbage bouldering circuit taking in the likes of the *Banana Finger* problems, the thuggy classic *Wednesday Climb*, the debilitating roof crack of *Definitive 5.11*, and the airy footless moves of *Life in a Radioactive Dustbin*, making a fantastically varied fast-access session in a small area.

But a real highlight of the circuit is reaching *All Quiet on the Eastern Front*. Here the quality really ramps up a notch or two. The elegant rib gained from the left by fingery moves, a brief pause, then build the feet high before confidently executing the long locks above. Superb hard rough rock, not quite as polished as the first few buttresses, tall enough to make you concentrate, and never taken too lightly. Add on the direct standing and sitting versions if you have the time and the skin, but save a little for the last sprint up *Remergence* in the fading light. Magic, just magic. Scatter my ashes here please.

An after-work crag par excellence; Andy Emery on *All Quiet*.

BURBAGE NORTH

 ## Cleo's Edge

If there was ever an ideal problem to launch a bouldering career with, then it's this. *Cleo's Edge* sits nestled in a cluster of three blocks, offering only a handful of problems, yet they manage to form a microcosm of problem styles across the grades.

The famous and savagely hard skin destroyer *Voyager*, along with its low start, remains close to the cutting edge, but from there we can trace our way down through the grades; classics on the largest boulder include the gently leaning fingery wall of *Giza*, the airy and spectacular highball jamming of *The Sphinx*, and the friendlier slabby sidewall. Right again, a fierce hanging mantel on to an obvious jug remains a local test piece. The true connoisseur visiting with a few pads and a reliable spotter may even be able to tame the rarely climbed *Sputnik*.

For the climber beginning their journey, *Cleo's* demands a little balance, a little gritstone 'feel' – even the top-out is no formality. Perhaps that's why old hands will enjoy returning to this classic time and time again.

Cleo's is always an undiluted pleasure – Andy Emery (above) and Jinalee De Silva (opposite).

BURBAGE NORTH

7a+ Boyager

At busy, popular crags there's usually an assumption that everything has been found, everything of value has already been done – the crag is 'worked out'. But time and time again it turns out not to be the case. These boulders in the woods of Burbage North are definitely testament to the power of the humble bouldering pad to unlock otherwise unclimbable rock. *Boyager* in particular is, or rather was, a fairly necky undertaking, but the recent accumulation of dead wood in what used to be the gaping coffin-sized hole masquerading as a landing has greatly improved things. Still, you'll want to arrive armed with a couple of pads, and make sure your hamstrings are warmed up before embarking on the full-bodied heelhooking and compression moves.

Along with the problems on the block immediately below – the best being *Monochrome* and *Mono Bulge* – there's plenty of steep and powerful bouldering to be enjoyed in the mid 7s here, all in a very modern, physical style. The downhill face of the block is beautifully rippled, but the rock quality of the flakes lets it down somewhat, as the sheer volume of glue keeping the holds on demonstrates. Don't pull too hard!

Left and right Frances Bensley makes short work of *Boyager*.
Centre The author on *Monochrome* circa the first ascent.

BURBAGE SOUTH

 7a+ ## The Alliance

Above Late summer evenings can offer surprisingly good conditions, at least enough for Tom Briggs on *The Alliance*.
Opposite Adam Long on *Thick End of the Wedge* in the depths of winter.

The easternmost part of Burbage South, nicknamed 'Burbage Earl' due to the similarity to its gritstone cousin near Skipton, was once something of a hidden gem for the Peak boulderer. Tucked away beyond the iconic hard routes of *Parthian Shot* and *Equilibrium*, the area competes with the best on quality if not quantity, and as such these days the cat is well and truly out of the bag.

Strong arête lines are a Burbage Earl speciality, with *The Rib*, *Desparête* and *Home Cooking* being legitimate classics, and the more recently unearthed *Thick End of the Wedge* rightly getting a lot of praise. It's tough to single out one particular problem, but *The Alliance* is understandably the most popular: quality compression moves with plenty of interest, the only fly in the ointment being the landing, but for the most part it's manageable. Some would argue that the sit start is even better – just be sure to save a bit of juice for the top-out.

BURBAGE SOUTH

 Sidepull Arch

Perceived wisdom at Burbage South states that the friendly boulder field below the crag is where the low-grade bouldering is at, and the dark brooding crag itself is reserved for the harder stuff. Broadly speaking this is true, and the boulders remain a classic venue for bouldering at the easier end of the spectrum, despite now sporting numerous deteriorating bullet-hole hand and footholds. The valley was used extensively for military target practice during World War II, but the boulder field below Burbage South took the brunt of the punishment. However, the crag itself was largely unscathed, and doesn't just offer hard problems. There are still plenty of great low-to-mid lines dotted along the crag, they just require a little more legwork.

On the *Sidepull Arch* wall, an unusually fortunate piece of quarrying has left us with a unique feature, and what's more the rock is surprisingly rough under the fingers by quarried grit's standards. Slabby at first, rearing up steeply to finish, it's an excellent test of footwork and finger strength at the grade. What's more, it's a surprisingly fruitful spot to get creative and conjure up endless variations as confidence increases – going up with the other hand, missing holds out or trying the variation problem just to the left. It's easy to lose half an hour here just fooling around, but it is never time wasted, as there's plenty to learn about friction, footwork and body position on this tiny canvas.

The next stop on a mid-grade circuit is invariably the fine-but-almost-ruined arête of *The Celtic Cross* (try doing it without touching any of the crumbling footholds) and after that the *7Ball* area has a bunch of great lines, culminating in the often-missed *Birch Tree Arête*. But just by *Sidepull Arch*, just across the quarried zawn of the Millwheel Wall bay, lies Jerry Moffatt's *Zorev*. This is one of the finest hard problems on quarried grit, a formidable mix of basic pulling with a bit of technique and spice thrown in, and not to be missed for anyone looking for a stern test of finger strength.

Laurie Smith on *Sidepull Arch* (opposite), Toby Wilson climbs a left-hand variant (top), and *The Celtic Cross* (bottom).

HIGGAR TOR

 The Big Slab

PEAK DISTRICT

With its iconic profile visible from afar, Higgar Tor's most famous feature from a climber's point of view is the brutal Leaning Block.* Notoriously in-your-face routes eschew the usual gritstone delicateness and rightly take centre stage, although Higgar is not to be typecast, as around the ramparts of the Tor there are boulder problems of all styles.

Higgar boasts a great utility circuit of easy-to-mid-grade highballs, which is invaluable in summer when the wind switches to a warm continental easterly and the shade is welcome. Working around the Tor clockwise, the climber will emerge into the last light of the evening at the jumble of blocks south of the Leaning Block, where *The Big Slab* dominates. Skin may be wearing thin by this point, but it can't be missed. Don't let the low grade fool you though, it manages to sustain interest all the way up. Once more before the midges emerge? Why not.

*Higgar's other notable feature is its spelling, being something of a sure-fire tell to identify a climber; the OS map and the rest of the non-climbing pubic opt for 'Higger'.

Steve Royle employs a cool head on *The Big Slab* (opposite) and wrestles the slopers of *Piss* (top right). Emma Banks on the rarely climbed *Krush Regime* (above).

145

MILLSTONE

Technical Master

In the film *Stone Monkey*, Johnny Dawes climbs *Technical Master* in trainers, Reebok Classics no less, over a decade before bouldering pads were available. I, on the other hand, have the latest rock shoes; these slick, polished footholds should feel better than this. I have a thick bouldering mat; the landing should not feel this hard and this far away. I have spent countless hours dangling off a piece of wood above my kitchen doorway; these arête holds ought to feel better than they do today. I should not feel this gripped.

I hate this – it doesn't make sense. Just as the crudely excavated, thirty-metre-high tottering quarry of Millstone Edge does not make any sense as a bouldering venue, *Technical Master* should not be a classic. It should not momentarily click into perfect focus and feel amazing. I should not be feeling this pleased with myself; I should not be buzzing like this. I definitely should not be chalking up to do it a second time. It doesn't make any sense, except that in that moment it kind of does.

Heels low, stay focused – Andy Emery shows the way.

MOTHER'S PET ROCK

7a+ Pet Cemetery

A glutton for mantel punishment, David Mason makes no excuses.

Everyone loves mantelshelves, right? Ha! This isn't going to be a runaway popular choice, because, if we're honest, most of us will go to the ends of the earth to avoid the humiliation of being shut down by an innocuous mantel problem. It pays to get your excuses lined up in advance. 'Actually I've got a bit of a dodgy elbow so I'll sit this one out' is a reliable option. 'Skin feeling a bit thin; gonna save myself for [insert problem name here] later on.' Or a personal favourite: 'Yeah this is nice light, just going to get some photos of you guys on it … oh is that the time?'

The problem with this strategy is the mantels will sit there taunting you, nagging you. They've been around for thousands of years so they're happy to wait. Time is on their side. They know you'll be back eventually. When you least expect it, when your guard is down, you'll find yourself trying one again. Why? Because you feel that insecurity burning within you, that hole in your climbing repertoire. Secretly you would *love* to be the sort of climber who calmly and confidently flips up on to palms on a highball, slopey mantel with ease. Not enough to actually do any specific training for it though. Maybe this time all that finger-boarding you've been doing will help …

Pet Cemetery at least does offer some tricky conventional moves to get established on the slopey top section, which help to usher you along a little – a warm-up for the inevitable sloper-mauling which awaits. Just get rocked over as far as possible then, with a bit of luck, you'll be committed to the mantel before you realise what's happening, before you have time to change your mind.

The other factor *Pet Cemetery* has in its favour is a superb local circuit you can fall back on to massage a dented ego – *Conan The Librarian*, the Mother Cap Quarry problems and Over Owler Tor should ensure you don't leave empty handed. For those who tackle *Pet Cemetery* with ease, *Mother's Pride*, just to the left, should be next on the agenda.

FROGGATT

7c Les Grand Doigts

A latterday classic. Ben Bransby (opposite; © **Adam Long**) and Char Williams (above; © **Adam Long**).

Heading north from the *Strapadictomy* area, where Froggatt's big route buttresses cease to be continuous, the edge line becomes more broken. From here all the way to the Hairpin Boulder by the parking lay-by there are scattered boulders and isolated buttresses and bays tucked away in the woods. Over the last decade or so these have begun to be explored in a concerted manner by boulderers, uncovering a range of worthwhile problems, and at the time of writing still hold many possibilities for those willing to put the time in to explore and clean new lines.

Marking the beginning of this recent wave of development, the big bald arête of *Les Grand Doigts* by Jamie Lilleman was instantly recognised as something a little special; popular but no pushover, it remains one of the most sought-after problems in the woods at Froggatt. The landing is a little improved these days, thankfully, although a particularly wild dismount would still be not advised. The sequence is absorbing, technical and delicate, not to mention frustrating. Expect to feel quite pleased with yourself after this one.

FROGGATT

8a+ Ill Behaviour

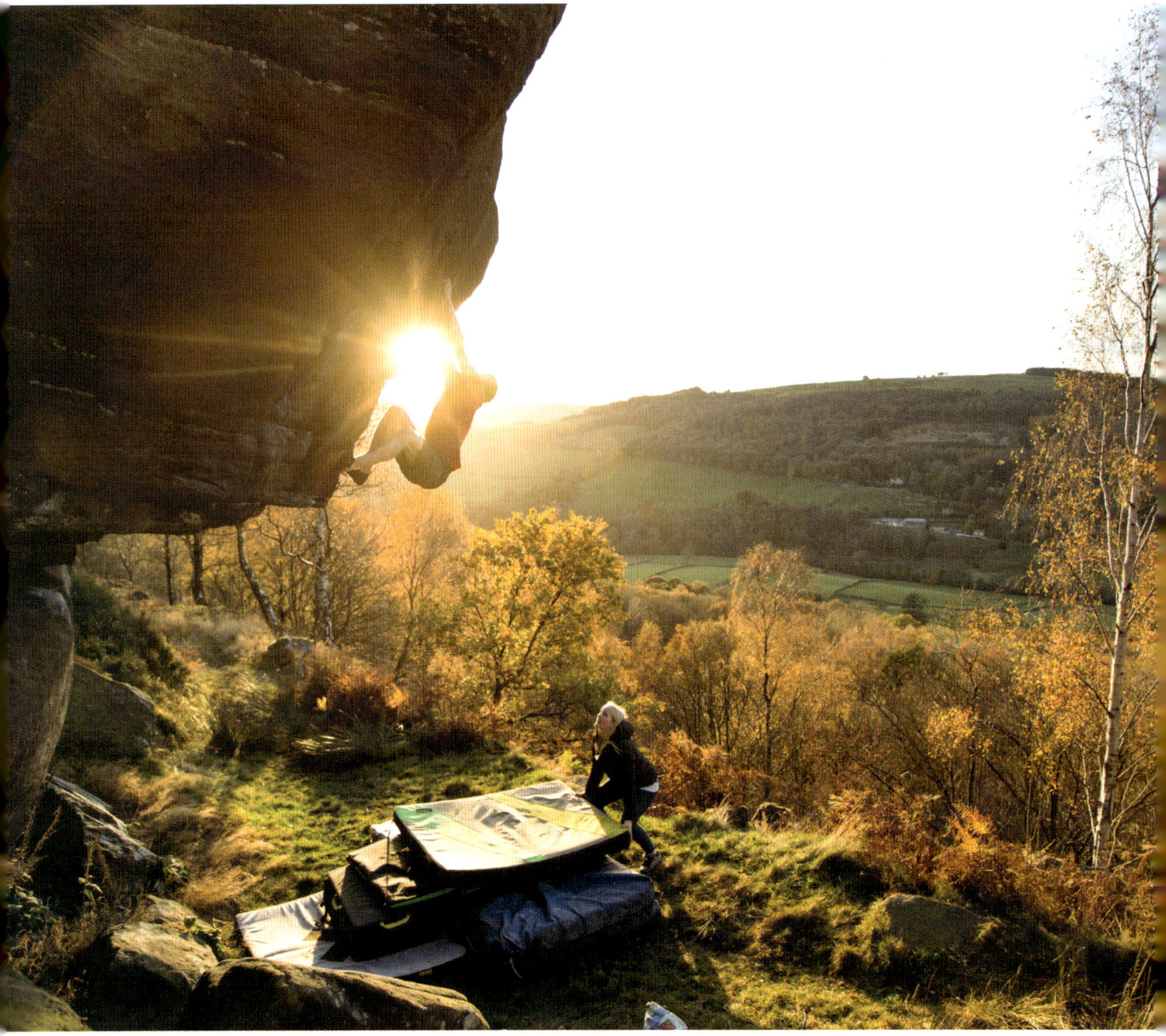

On a boulder with only three major lines on it, choosing one for inclusion in this book ought to be easy. However, when those three include the classics *Renegade Master* and *The Screaming Dream*, things become less clear cut. Each line on this huge block has its own unique history and place in Peak climbing folklore. Mark Leach's epic siege on *Screaming* is the stuff of legends, and Jerry Moffatt taking his bouldering power and applying it to the steep right-hand side cemented his superstar status. However, both of these lines were routes rather than boulder problems from their inception. *Screaming* has ample gear on it, rendering bouldered ascents a choice born out of stylistic considerations or convenience rather than out of necessity. *Renegade* is routinely bouldered out these days, although almost always taking a right-hand finish which differs from the original solution.

For this reason, Ned Feehally's *Ill Behaviour* from 2017 gets the pick here. Straight up the middle of the block, and where *Renegade* slinks right just blast straight up for the top with a gut-wrenching dyno from poor holds, with a huge fall awaiting if you don't latch the top. At the upper limit in terms of both height and commitment but, crucially, also quality. It remains an unambiguous statement of pure bouldering audacity. Well worth standing underneath this one day just to get your head around it.

Back once again, Ned Feehally winds up and explodes skyward. (Left © **Nick Brown**; right © **Adam Long**.)

FROGGATT

7a+ Hot Toddy

Tody's Playground has something for everyone. Mina Leslie-Wujastyk sets to work while David and Isaac Mason provide moral support.

PEAK DISTRICT

Problems that top out are actually quite rare at the main crag area of Froggatt. Locals have long since recognised this as a boon in poor winter weather, because a full session can be had without ever having to go anywhere near the wet or snowy crag top. There's plenty to be done that stays dry or otherwise dries very rapidly, sheltered from chilling northerlies. Should things brighten up, Froggatt is a lovely winter suntrap; T-shirt weather in January is not unheard of. But jump-off problems, or ones that leave the boulderer effectively soloing a route either up or down to get back to safety, aren't to everyone's liking. In *Hot Toddy,* it's great to have an option for a true top-quality top-out problem at an achievable grade.

The Tody's Playground buttress is in itself a little oasis, tucked away from the rest of the crag. With a lovely set of lower-grade problems, perfect landings and separate from the passing traffic of the rest of the crag, it's a great spot for families with young children. *Hot Toddy* then provides the little sting in its tail to test mum and dad's muscles,

although it's worth knowing that it's missing from older guides as the left end of Tody's Playground used to be obscured by a tree, long since fallen down. This opened up the possibility of a problem through the steepness everyone had glanced at, but was previously inaccessible. Dan Varian swooped in, and *Hot Toddy* was born. Thankfully this one isn't as desperate as most of Dan's additions to British bouldering.

As the problem has matured and received more ascents, it's almost morphed into two problems for the price of one – both equally entertaining but in contrasting styles. The most common method is to stay left all the way, under the steepness, where compression moves, slaps and heelhooks lead to good finishing holds over to the left on the back arête. But after the first few moves it's also possible to go more directly and then stay right on a rising rib feature for a completely different, more delicate finish. Which is better? Do both. Check 'em out and make a direct comparison.

CURBAR

7b The Art of White Hat Wearing

We often like to think that grit problems come ready made, off the peg. You just need to find them, give them a light brush, and off you go. But local activists and developers often find potential new lines where the landing needs 'sorting out', sometimes involving considerable effort. Usually this is fairly uncontroversial and, for the most part, unseen work. But the issue becomes more complicated when existing trad routes, often established before the advent of bouldering mats, get the same treatment.

The Art of White Hat Wearing is a case in point. Andy Crome's audacious E5 6c route from 1992 was largely ignored until the removal of a large block from the landing, and subsequent retro-patio work. While patioing and landing work was not always universally lauded at the time, the route was transformed into a high-quality highball problem and very quickly became one of the most popular in the Peak, and one of the best at the grade on quarried gritstone full stop.

It's hard to dispute that *TAOWHW* is now a completely different proposition than the first ascent, but then again, the same is true for every route or problem making use of new gear – pads, cams or sticky rubber, to name but a few. Certainly there aren't many ascentionists clamouring to have the original bad landing reinstated, so at least for now prevailing opinion seems to have settled the matter. But who knows how these routes will be viewed through the lens of future trends? Maybe dangerous short routes climbed without pads will come into fashion? Maybe top roping will replace pad use to reduce ground erosion? Stranger things have happened. After all, who would have dreamed we'd all be carrying 150 litres of foam on our backs to go climbing?

Jon Fullwood on Curbar's other *'Art of ... '*, in this case *Japan* (top left). Kim Leyland (opposite) and John Coefield (bottom left) enjoying *White Hat*.

CURBAR

8-ish Smiling Buttress

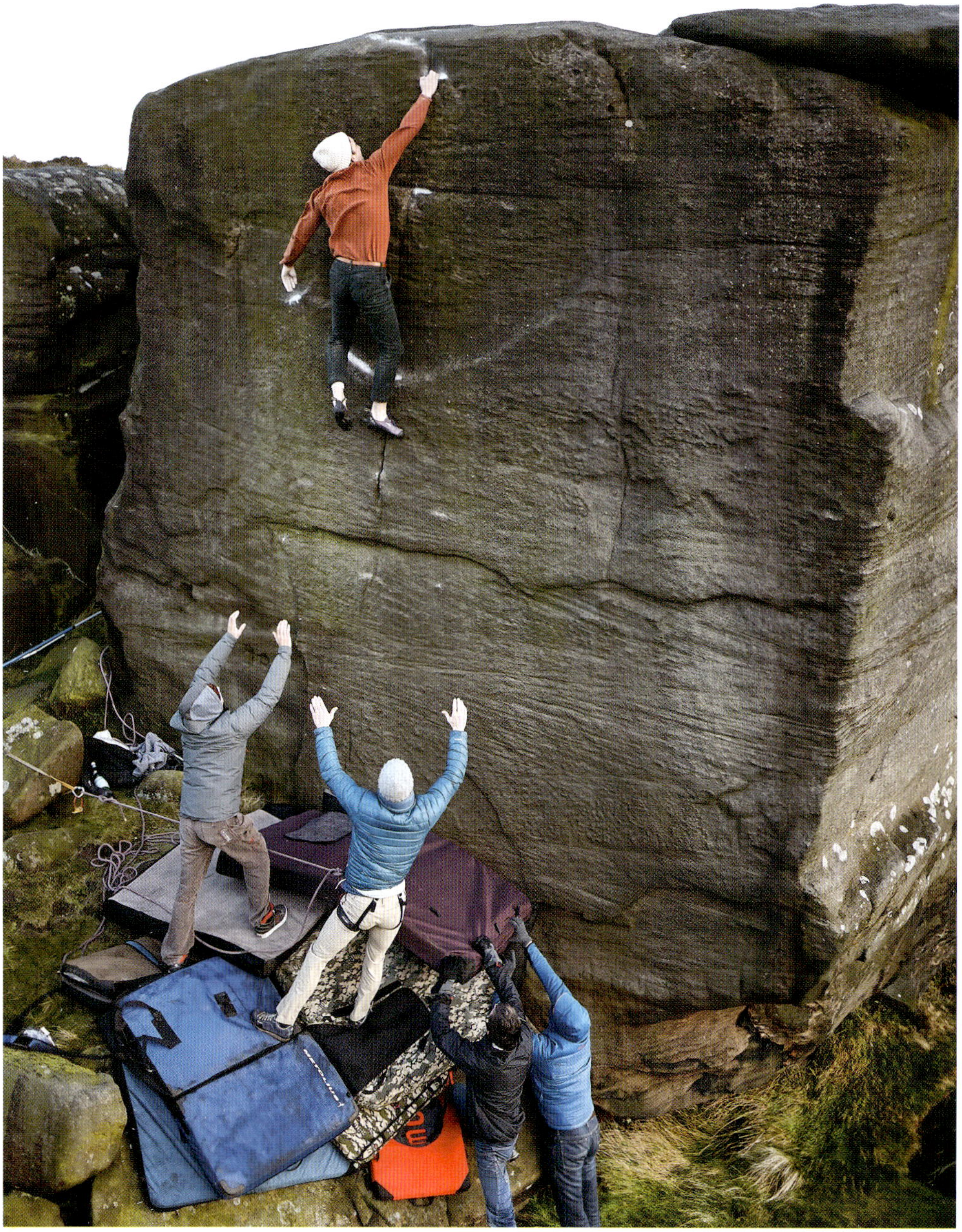

There is inevitably a concern that the problems selected to appear in a book like this just become magnets for puerile tickers, catnip for the bouldering consumerists, logbook entries to accumulate. Well, if *Ill Behaviour* or *Lanny Bassham* didn't stop them in their tracks then this one surely will.

An unashamedly elitist inclusion, and unrepeated at the time of writing, Tyler Landman's audacious solution to this well-known 'last great problem' is the crystallisation of everything gritstone can be. A pure line straight up the middle of a beautiful blank wall; brick hard, condition dependent, technical and high, but relatively approachable. At least the necky, final move is over quickly, one way or another.

Tyler's 2013 ascent remains one of the most magnificent pieces of climbing I've ever witnessed. As a testament to how well Tyler climbed it, immediately afterwards there were unmistakable psyched glances exchanged among the assembled spotters and photographers, as is often the case when you see someone make a hard problem look steady. As if your mate had just knocked off a nice highball 7b so you might as well have a go. Luckily we all came to our senses before the shoes and chalk came out, and we left with egos intact, happy to have just witnessed a truly special episode in gritstone history.

For the rest of us mere mortals, the closest equivalent to *Smiling Buttress* is the neighbouring *Art of Japan*. The outlook is identical, being a fine-grained north-facing wall perched right up on the wildest battlements of Curbar Edge. Exposed and quick to dry, it's an excellent problem and, being almost a full two number grades easier than *Smiling*, it's one a few more of us can enjoy. If you've got the time and a few pads there's a great extended highballing circuit up here – *Rise of the Robots*, *Fidget*, *Lifeseeker*, *Dog-Leg Crack* and *The Unreachable Star* to name a few are all superb.

Tyler Landman on *Smiling Buttress's* first, and at the time of writing, only, ascent. (Above © **Adam Long**.)

CURBAR

5+ Curbar Corner

Dave Norton on the arête of *Neat* (above) and *Curbar Corner* (top), also climbed ably by George Norton (opposite).

It's reassuring that even at a crag as intimidating and uncompromising as Curbar, fine easier problems can still be found. Offering some respite from the huge, steep and hard buttresses which proliferate at Curbar, the relatively friendly area of slabs around *Curbar Corner* would be more at home at Froggatt. The corner itself remains an enjoyable old classic, often overlooked and no pushover, but a reliable favourite for those in the know.

It provides entry to a great circuit of problems in the vicinity – variations on and around each arête of the corner being the obvious next step, notably the more recent *Jamie and His Magic Torch* providing a frustrating test of gritstone knack. For those happy to venture a little higher, the immaculate highball pocket-work of *Finger Distance*, slap bang up the centre of the main slab, is not to be missed, along with the less technical but much bolder *El Vino Collapso*. For the bold with a lot of pads it's not out of the question to 'boulder out' the hard classic route *White Water* – but be warned, the crux is at the very top.

BASLOW

6b · A Beagle Too Far

Once completely overlooked, Baslow has really matured over recent years into a bouldering venue to properly compete with its neighbours Curbar and Gardom's. A great evening venue in the spring or autumn, on the crag itself there's a mixture of fine quarried and natural lines, so you can have your pick of mid-grade highball technical walls, short steep problems and traverses, with a few good harder lines thrown in.

One of the Eastern Edges' absolute standout boulders, much has been written about an ascent of the Eagle Stone being a traditional rite of passage for the young men of the area. The summit retains an air of exclusivity even today, and as such any problem on here would be a contender for inclusion in this book. What the Eagle Stone lacks in quantity it makes up for with the quality of its independent stand-up lines. Just the right height, good landings, excellent rock quality, and what's more just that special something that's hard to quantify. *A Beagle Too Far* gets the nod for being a true line of least resistance and hence very satisfying, but most climbers won't find too much to complain about on the rest of the harder 7s either.

On the crag itself, Baslow's weakness is the rock quality – it is not always bullet-hard gritstone. Expect the odd crispy edge on the quarried problems, and some of the notable, natural problems – *Flatworld* being a prime example – are suffering a little where high popularity and less than premium rock quality coincide. There's still plenty with good quality rock to seek out though, like the enjoyable slab of *Renaissance*. Fortunately, being at the easier end of the scale means it's amenable enough that every ascent isn't preceded by the traffic of hundreds of failed attempts, so it remains a bit of a guilt-free pleasure.

The author on *A Beagle Too Far* (opposite and bottom left); John Coefield enters its rounded groove (top left) and Tom Crane on the technical *Renaissance* (middle left).

GRIT BLOCS

GARDOM'S

7c I Like Ya Cut G

The main crag at Gardom's is a bit of a slow burner for bouldering. Lacking the obvious easy-access famous (and now a little worn looking) problems around *Mark's Roof* and *8 Ball* on the North Boulders, the crag itself rewards a bit of extra effort. Over the last twenty or so years problems have been steadily added, boulders cleaned, buttresses developed, future classics uncovered. At the time of writing there's a pretty rich extended circuit covering the entire length of the crag, dotted between the classic trad routes, and there's still plenty more to come.

I Like Ya Cut G is a problem that typifies the Gardom's experience – quiet, easily overlooked, and completely absorbing. A recent addition by Jon Fullwood, this unusual overlapping wall takes no prisoners and has been known to see off some of grit's biggest hitters. Fiercely crimpy, with a bit of weird tech undercutting thrown in, it somehow manages to be simultaneously slabby and overhanging. Come equipped with good skin on a cloudy day, otherwise expect to have a torrid time of it.

Close by you'll find some of the many isolated classics, old and new. Perhaps the slopey tussle of *Pogle's Wood*, the basic yarding of *Perfect Day Direct Start*, or the innocuous but fantastic *Bad/Angry Fox*. From there, if skin allows, you might work southwards – take your pick from *2020 Vision, A Fearful Orange, Drum Roll, Plan D*, or *English Voodoo*. Take a brush and a couple of pads to get the best out of the circuit.

Martin Smith (above) and Ben Bransby (opposite, bottom) unpick the weird crimpy technicalities of *I Like Ya Cut G*. The author (opposite, top) on *Bad/Angry Fox*.

PEAK DISTRICT

GRIT BLOCS

GARDOM'S

6b+ G-Thang

The little wooded area at the far southern end of Gardom's Edge feels delightfully out of the way – not too many walkers, not enough problems to really attract the hordes, yet enough traffic for most problems to remain clean. The shapely groove of *G-Thang* gives every impression of a technical challenge. However, as it turns out the climbing is actually fairly basic – for a gritstone groove – albeit not at the expense of the quality of the movement.

The only downside is it feels like it's over too quickly, hence it's one of those problems that it's hard to walk away from having only climbed it once. The sit start variations, both with and without the right arête, provide extra sport, without detracting from the no-holds-barred stand-up line. Pull on and blast up for the top – then do it again.

For aspiring hardpersons, the southern end of Gardom's is also home to Ned Feehally's more recent test piece *Dhalsim*. This brilliant leaning wall is becoming something of a modern classic, graded 8a+ off the deck, but a higher 7b+ start also exists off the block to the right – *Pit Fighter* – and is worth seeking out.

Above, opposite top John Coefield on *G-Thang* (opposite top © **Adam Long**).
Far left John Coefield on *Plan D*.
Left Martin Mobråten eyes up the final move on *Suavito*.

GRIT BLOCS

MOORSIDE ROCKS

8a+ Superbloc

The finale of the Gardom's Edge escarpment, the last significant rock before the crag-top track descends to the pub and car park, Moorside Rocks pack a punch. For many years, John Allen's *The Jackalope*, a just-about-highballable flared crack, was the main event, but that has been eclipsed by Miles Gibson's *Superbloc* from 2003.

Originally given E8, this proud rounded arête with long monkey-on-a-stick moves on poor holds is now regarded as 'only' a highball, although plenty of ascentionists still opt to work the slopey top-out moves on a rope first. Needless to say, cold crisp conditions are mandatory. Arguably this is really best considered a hybrid route, but however you choose to classify it one thing is certain: that it's one of the finest of the genre, whatever that genre is.

Superbloc also has the attraction of being one of the more amenable of Gibson's hard contributions to gritstone, with lines like the bold *Dangermouse* E9 at Wimberry and the less dangerous but still bloody hard *Fagus Sylvatica* E8 at Burbage still awaiting repeats at the time of writing; in the case of the latter, it's twenty years and counting.

No stranger to gritstone, Michele Caminati milks the fingertip slopers of *Superbloc*. © Michele Caminati

GRIT BLOCS

BIRCHEN EDGE

7b+ **HMS Daring**

Birchen Edge is a crag often disparaged as simply being a 'punter's crag' – although it has to be said, it's a brilliant punter's crag. As such, it didn't attract much attention from boulderers until relatively recently. *HMS Daring* is by far the pick of that crop of development. Technical, slopey, a great sequence of moves, high enough to concentrate the mind but not really dangerous – it's up there with the best of its genre.

Immediately to the left is the John Allen route *Gritstone Megamix* from 1984, another high, slopey tussle now tamed by bouldering pads at 7a. Combined with the other problems which dot the crag, Birchen is a great venue for a group visit with a few pads. Winter remains your best bet for decent friction on the dark rock, making the most of the sheltered aspect, with a warm fire and a beverage of your choice waiting for you at the pub afterwards. An absolute belter.

Jon Fullwood completes an early repeat of *HMS Daring* (opposite; © John Coefield). John Coefield on the marginal slopey crimps of *Jumpers for Trousers* (above right) and Andy Harris on *Gritstone Megamix* (above left).

GRIT BLOCS

DUKE'S SEAT

7b Darkthrone

We see time and time again that gritstone has a habit of churning out highly technical, classic, vertical 7b and 7b+ problems, often ribs or arêtes, sometimes a little highball. Maybe this is something to do with the geology and topography of the average crag, or maybe because that grade lies at a bit of a sweet spot: attainable by many with some effort and application, yet still hard enough to not be completely trivial even for very strong climbers. Maybe the fact that taller problems tend to linger long in the memory plays a part in this phenomenon? Either way, *Darkthrone* is very much up there with the likes of *West Side Story, Spare Rib, Lay-by Arête, Fight on Black, Ben's Groove* and *HMS Daring*.

Sitting at the southern end of the Chatsworth Estate, tucked away unnoticed in the woods, Duke's Seat had to wait until 2017 to see development as a serious bouldering venue, and since then a revolving cast of local activists has contributed with various gems unearthed from obscurity, but Mark Rankine really snatched the prized line with *Darkthrone*. Climbed exclusively on slopey holds, *Darkthrone* is best enjoyed in cool conditions; luckily, as the woods are fairly open, it actually catches a decent breeze, making pouncing upon a dry winter's day not impossible. Far from being a one-hit wonder, the woods offer enough problems to keep most of us busy for a few sessions. Being a debilitating thirty-minute flat walk from the road, it tends to scare off the fair-weather boulderer, so it's a delightfully quiet spot. Conversely, don't expect to turn up to find a huge pad stack and spotters in situ, you'll have to muster your own team. But with the promise of a cool breezy spring afternoon with the low sunlight raking through the trees, your friends shouldn't take much persuading.

Jim Pope finds just enough friction on *Darkthrone* on an early summer morning.

ROACHES UPPER TIER

7c Proper Gander

The most iconic of all the climbing spots in Staffordshire, the Roaches has always been the touchstone for climbing on this side of the Peak. The mothership: overseeing the climbing scene much like Stanage does in the east, or Almscliff in the north.

There's a remarkable variability in the rock itself over quite a limited area; from the bullet-hard flat grey rock of the Far Skyline and the Five Clouds, to the softer pink bulbous Lower Tier boulders. The Upper Tier boulders in particular are distinct from the other areas in polishing up very readily, as can be seen on the ever-popular old classic *Joe's Arête*. But there's still plenty of new things being uncovered.

Round to the south of the Upper Tier lies *Proper Gander*, where Jon Fullwood found an inventive solution to the unassuming bulges, pinches and slopers that trace the least dangerous line up this huge, rippled block. This is full-bodied gritstone weirdness cranked up to the max. Overhead heels and kneebars will lead with some contortion to a bit of a breather at half height before commencing battle with the most grit-like of top-outs – subtle, slopey and high. Worth a brush before you embark, but at least you probably won't have to queue for it.

An unlikely modern classic, Jon Fullwood shows how it's done with kneebar wizardry.

THE FIVE CLOUDS

7a+ Hard Arête

The bouldering at the Clouds, it has to be said, is limited in terms of sheer numbers, but in terms of quality there's no ceiling. *Hard Arête* is a great line in itself, and it forms the key problem to a range of other sit starts and finishes. The entire block appears beautifully sculpted by nature. Handful after handful of sugar-textured rock, fortuitously deposited beneath the crag, it continues to attract boulderers from far afield. Although anyone driving over on the promise of a classic 'nice sunny day' might find themselves cursing the conditions as the Five Clouds, despite their name, are something of a suntrap, even in the depths of winter.

Hard Arête will win no prizes for imaginative problem naming, but it is at least accurate. It's deceptively complex, packing in a lot of climbing in its short length – indeed you may have to do a toehook move before you've even left the ground. And the easy top-out section after the inconveniently oriented flake often turns out to be anything but. Add on the sit start moves of *Tetris* and it turns into even more of a battle at 7c. Likewise, the extended *Four Lions* 7b+ leftward finish will leave you wishing you'd climbed the initial problem more efficiently. The slopey *Columns* at 7c+ will likely feel desperate in anything but cold, shady conditions.

It's not all hard though, the slab *Trust* is good value if an honest approach is taken – avoid grabbing the right arête too soon. Just up the hill, *Matchbox Slab* is an unmissable 5+. Bring your blinkers to resist the temptation to reach rightwards and you'll be rewarded with some of the purest friction work available at the grade. Just superb.

Opposite John Coefield, Adam Coefeld and Jon Fullwood (clockwise from top) on *Hard Arête* in different seasons. (Opposite top © **Adam Long**.) **Above** the author smearing on *Matchbox Slab*.

THE FIVE CLOUDS

6b Finger of Fate

Jon Fullwood (above) and Hazel Findlay (right; © **Adam Long**) on the immaculate rock of this tall arête.

The Five Clouds really has too many prime chunks of compact immaculate grit for a crag this size. You could be forgiven for believing pretty much every notable problem here is a classic, and you'd not be far wrong. Even ignoring the aforementioned *Hard Arête* boulder for a second, there's the weird thumb-press rockover on *Milky Buttons*, savage blind seam crimping on *Who Needs Ready Brek?*, the juggy highball laybacking of *Communist Crack*, and the steep, modern *The Imperfect Catch* and *The Darkest Cloud*. Rest assured that a fine crisp winter's day out at the Five Clouds with a few friends is something really special.

Finger of Fate is without a doubt one of the finest arêtes of its grade you'll find anywhere. Given 6b, or old school E1, the grade is sort of irrelevant as the inevitable draw of the line makes it a difficult one to walk past, whatever your standard. The landing isn't as user-friendly as it could be, which sharpens the mind a little. It feels airy as soon as you commit to smears and open handfuls of Staffordshire's finest, with the landing rolling away beneath your feet. A bit of faith in friction is soon rewarded with decent holds as the diagonal crack falls to hand.

A glance leftwards across the grey sweep of steep slab reveals the possibility of a very hard project line up the slab for those capable of high-angle smearing while pulling on not very much. The old problem *Nadin's Secret Finger* gains what would be the final few moves of this super project from around the left arête, a little up the grassy bank. At one time it was widely assumed this actually took the slab direct, no doubt further cementing Simon Nadin's already legendary status in these parts. Still, his rarely climbed indirect solution at 7c will be hard enough for most.

NTH CLOUD

6b Swivel Finger

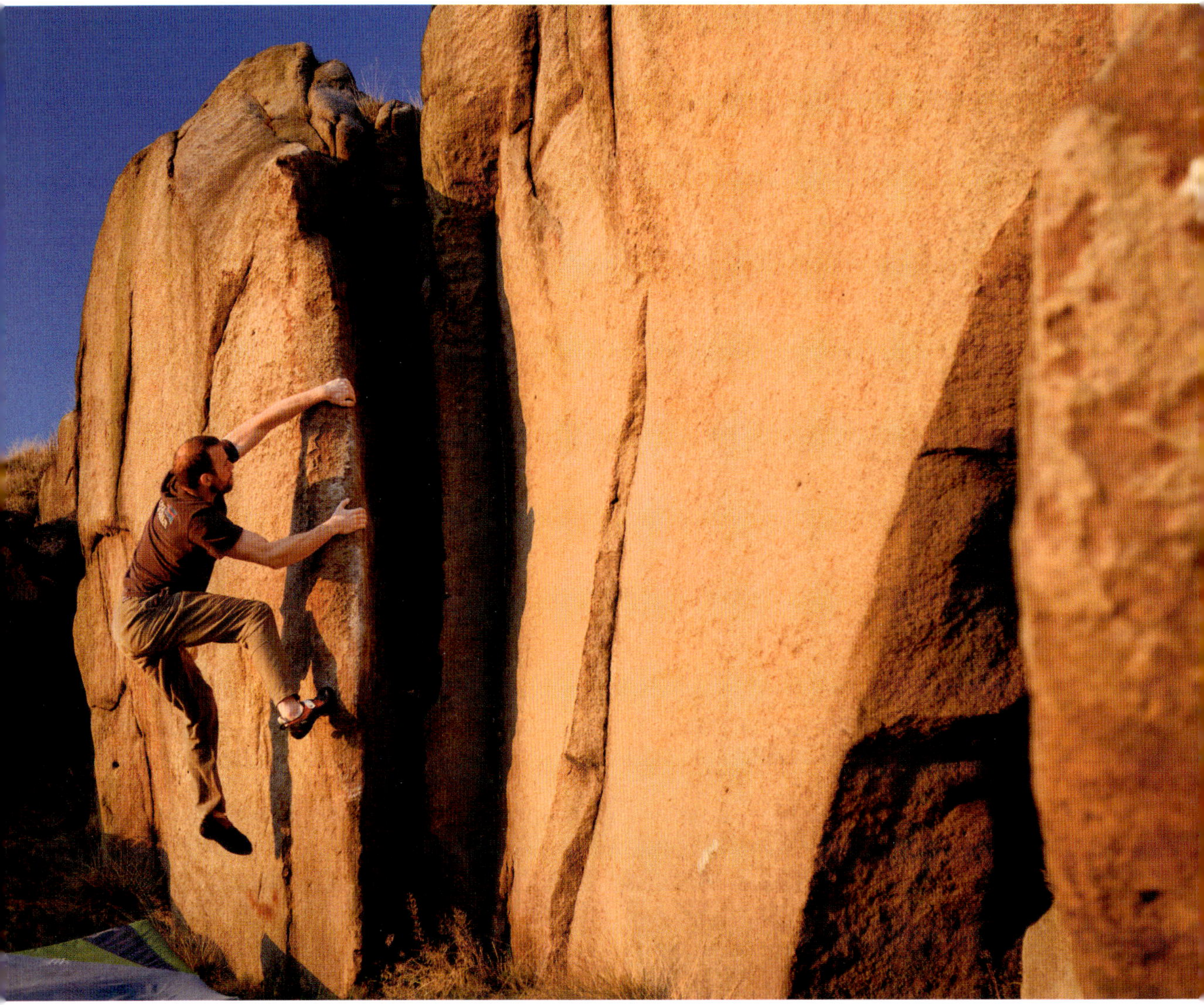

Ned Feehally holding the barn-door open to let the last light of day in.

The spiritual cousin of the Five Clouds, a stone's throw away but requiring a completely separate approach, the rock of Nth Cloud bears all the hallmarks of the very best of the Staffordshire area. Rough grippy grey rock with a slight salmon-pink tinge that almost seems to glow neon cerise in the setting winter sun. Like its neighbours, the quality is condensed into just a handful of trad and bouldering lines, but what lines they are.

For sheer purity of form, *Swivel Finger* cannot be faulted. Ungenerously it only has one hold with which to cover about four and a half metres of ground – the arête itself. By any metric it ought not to be enough. The climber is left to make up the shortfall with a sort of fleeting synergy of opposing forces. Keeping the body's centre of gravity in just the right place by pushing and pulling simultaneously, feet smearing hard, not too low, not too high, is the only option. With focus required right until the top, concentration and a bit of that magic gritstone 'feel' buys you just enough time to climb this thing without the barn-door swinging closed in your face. As a true test of technique, they don't come much better than this.

HEN CLOUD

6c+ Original Starlight and Storm

Although *Starlight and Storm* is often climbed on the right-hand side of the arête by convention, it seems the original line somehow slipped off the radar over the years. First climbed by the late gritstone legend John Allen, the left-hand solution to this leaning pinnacle below the intimidating bulk of the Hen Cloud crag has been relegated to a jump-or-traverse-off minor variation, and with it losing half the climbing. Hence, this feast of double-arête highball slapping has been hiding in plain sight for years. How did we let this happen?

Sharing a name with Gaston Rébuffat's beautiful lyrical account of his ascents of the six big north faces of the Alps during the 1930s and 1940s, what we will call *Original Starlight and Storm* perhaps lacks a little of the drama of this classic of Alpine literature, but it still has plenty of excitement condensed into its six metres of height. Indeed, most of us will be glad we're tackling this challenge in the bouldering mat era. Heelhooking moves on the rough slopers and pockets lead to an unhelpfully sparse breakline. From here on in, there's nothing left to it except run your feet up high, squeeze and commit. Pure John Allen magic.

For those in a highballing mindset, Hen Cloud does offer a few good challenges for those who can resist the charms of the crag's tremendous trad routes. Alongside the numerous splitter cracks, big bold walls and arêtes, *Touch* is the standout highball wall at 7a+, and *Easter Rising* is worth searching out at 6c.

Nic Sellars on the right-hand finish (top; © **Adam Long**), Ned Feehally on the left-hand solution (above and opposite).

NEWSTONES

 ## Charlie's Overhang

Just the right side of horror show, that's how I think of *Charlie's Overhang*. High slopey finishes around a roof on gritstone have a habit of turning nasty pretty quickly. Just one factor being out of balance can easily turn a highball into a soul-searching solo, or an all-out chop route. The scrittle could be too much for comfort, the landing a little awkward, retreat from the commitment point too involved. As luck would have it, *Charlie's* manages to stay just on the right side of all those pitfalls.

Trust me, save this one for a good day, with a fresh breeze, when you're feeling confident, that's probably the best way to savour it. It's easy enough to give the top holds a gentle brush for any errant scrittle from above, then give it one hundred per cent and be rewarded. Combined with the rest of the Newstones and Baldstones ridgeline there's a great circuit to be had (sadly some problems are a little worse for wear), but whatever grade you operate at *Charlie's* is sure to be one that lingers in the memory.

Below Adam Long about to throw a heel up and engage grovel mode.
Right Jon Fullwood working his way along the protrusions of *Ripple*.
© John Coefield

BALDSTONES

 Elephant's Ear

Utterly irresistible, the layback flake of *Elephant's Ear* is solid gold. Even if you're here to try the classic technical arête of *Clever Skin*, or the bunched rockover weirdness of *Fielder's Wall*, do not miss this one. Handful after handful of rough gritstone, grippy smears for feet, easy but not trivial, it's everything a lower-grade classic should be. It's a fitting conclusion to a couple of hours spent working along the ridge from Newstones, sampling the great circuit of mid-grade little classics.

The rock at Baldstones for the most part withstands traffic a little better than Newstones, but as always avoid unless absolutely one hundred per cent dry. The entire ridgeline faces east so doesn't get much sun to quickly dry the rock, but offers a bit of much needed shade in summer. When the wind switches to an easterly and the west-facing crags become midge-infested hellholes, it offers a welcome escape.

Mark Sharratt enjoying *Elephant's Ear* – always a pleasure. © Mark Sharratt

RAMSHAW ROCKS

7a+ Tierdrop

When approached from the east, the jagged claws of Ramshaw Rocks emerging from the hillside offer your first glimpse of Staffordshire gritstone. The crag is an intimidating spectacle, where brutal-looking, steep blank pinnacles abut awkward, wide fist-shredding cracks. You know in the pit of your stomach that this is one of those crags which is just itching to dish out an ego-bruising smackdown to any unsuspecting climber, one way or another.

It is with some relief that the boulderer can shirk these challenges, although for the most part the crag's drop-off type problems are a little unfulfilling. In *Tierdrop* however we have a truly brilliant problem which you don't have to be a complete masochist to enjoy. High, but nothing out of the ordinary, the line of positive and not-so-positive pinches leads to the lip and a final long pull to safety. Feel free to add on the very good sit start and go round again if you've got enough juice in the tank.

But don't leave Ramshaw without checking out the cluster of boulders centred around the excellent and often overlooked 6b named *The Pinches*, as here lies something of a local big three: the 'logue' problems – *Epilogue*, *Monologue* and *Dialogue* – are all excellent proud lines and not to be missed.

Opposite An outstanding highball, Ned Feehally rocks into the ancient carved runnel on *Tierdrop*. **Above** *The Pinches*.

GRIT BLOCS

ROBIN HOOD'S STRIDE

7b Big Al Qaeda

Fancy footwork unlocks *Big Al Qaeda* – Tom Schofield-Graham (top), Harry Pennells (bottom) and Jon Fullwood (opposite). © **Adam Long**

For such an obvious line at an enormously popular venue, *Big Al Qaeda* held out a long time, only receiving a first ascent at the hands of Michael Duffy in 2003. But our patience was rewarded.

This is one of the proudest lines at a crag with no shortage of aesthetic arêtes and bulging prows. It overhangs the sloping landing in an intimidating fashion, with an airy finish, so it's no surprise it held out until bouldering mats were commonplace. Most ascents will make liberal use of a sort of loose heel–toe scum over to the right, and a steely core, to momentarily check the swing long enough to reach up to the dish in the right-hand face. From here it's a sprint to the runnel around the arête and hence the top before strength or confidence fades.

If *Big Al* goes down without putting up too much of a fight, then take a look at the line just right again, using the hold in the face with the other hand; this is a 7c called *Osama Bin Yardin*. Great name.

Happily, the arête of this looming shield-shaped face was too futuristic for climbers of yesteryear so wasn't deemed worthy of the attention by the numerous chippers which have been something of a blight on The Stride and Cratcliffe over the years. Remarkably, chipping or vandalism one way or another has continued to happen here well into the 2010s, despite the rest of the Peak largely escaping this sort of unwanted attention.

GRIT BLOCS

CRATCLIFFE TOR

6a+ Egg Arête

The boulders at the top of Cratcliffe Tor have long been a favourite spot, with a completely different atmosphere to the Eastern Edges, and rock feeling reminiscent in shape and colour to Staffordshire grit. But sadly, many of the problems, particularly the easier lines, have suffered the same chipping fate as their neighbours at The Stride. Once pristine slabs and arêtes are now dotted with slots, scars and disintegrating footholds.

This vandalism is truly unfortunate, not just for immediate aesthetic reasons, but because it sets an inevitable chain of events into motion: at a popular venue like Cratcliffe the weaker exposed rock never has a chance to build up a patina again due to the constant traffic. A flavour of how good those problems might have been can however be found just down the hill beneath the trees.

A nugget of beautifully rounded Fontainebleau magic, somehow spared the wrath of the chisel, the star problem on The Egg boulder is the rounded main arête. Unassuming at first, it's best climbed on its right-hand side where a frustrating sloper maul and blind footholds will lead inevitably to a mantel of sorts. In inimitable gritstone style it should feel easy when it clicks, but impossible otherwise. On a really cold day try the problem immediately to the right for some truly improbable sloper alchemy.

No basic pulling here. John Coefield (above; © **Adam Long**) and Gwyneth Uttley (top and opposite).

CRATCLIFFE TOR

 ## Brain Dead

Around at the business end of Cratcliffe, beneath the main east-facing part of the crag, lies a very different arête to the previous problem. Feeling a million miles from the idyllic picnic-spot ambience of the crag-top boulders, *Brain Dead* sits in the shade, amongst the bracken and tortured boughs and branches. The boulder presumably once fell from the crag above eons ago, and now it almost seems as if an enormous hand is desperate to claw it back into the earth. But for the moment the trees are gracious enough to still allow it to be climbed, providing you don't bump your head topping out.

In stark contrast to the *Egg Arête*, this tall sharply cut arête takes a form we more often expect of quarried grit, if it wasn't for the rough texture reminding us that it could not be anything but completely natural. High and airy enough to focus the senses, but relatively straightforward, it can be climbed on either side at the same grade, so don't just settle for doing one. Each version has a slightly different character, with no real consensus as to which side is best. The debate rages on.

Rock the grip of nature; Gwyneth Uttley on both sides of *Brain Dead*.

STANTON MOOR

7b Spare Rib (Brutal Arête)

A side effect of the complete lack of documentation around bouldering on Stanton Moor was that once the 2000s bouldering boom took hold nobody was really sure what had been 'done before, youth'. Names, grades and first ascent claims changed hands at a faster rate than anyone could keep up with. This problem was eventually chalked up to legendary Peak boulderer Jason Myers, although it is unknown if either of the names associated with this problem originate from the first ascensionist.

Two matters pertaining to this problem have been settled by consensus. One is that *Spare Rib* is by far the better name. Second is that this is a truly outstanding problem. The side of this huge solid buttress is marked by set of compound arches in the rock, like someone dropped a handful of stones into a pond which then froze instantly. *Spare Rib* starts at the termination of these arches, but soon leaves the sanctuary of the wave feature and makes a break for the top.

Another in that long tradition of absolutely classic technical vertical gritstone 7b and 7b+ problems, *Spare Rib* also requires a little bit of commitment and belief to make the long move for the distant finishing holds. Although it has to be said 'finishing holds' is something of a misnomer, as you still have to mantel out the sloping lip, no straws to clutch at. You're not out of trouble until you're safely standing on top feeling very pleased with yourself.

Stanton Moor has plenty of other pearls if you don't mind a bit of walking around and exploring. Although the rock quality isn't universally bulletproof (see the Cork Stone for example), where it's good it's damn good. Usually, Font 6c+ is the worst grade in climbing, requiring ninety-nine per cent of the output of climbing Font 7a without any of the kudos, but nevertheless *Brad's Arête 'The Presence of Absence'* is worth the effort and one of the finest sub-7 problems in the southern Peak.

Above Char Williams on *Brad's Arête 'The Presence of Absence'.* © **Adam Long**
Opposite top and right the author and Adam Long on *Spare Rib*.
Opposite, bottom left just below lies the delightful *Little Brother*.

STANTON IN THE WOODS

6b Appliance Friction

For a rock type often characterised by delicate footwork and smearing moves at the limit of friction, it turns out that pure smearing slabs on gritstone are actually quite rare. That is to say there's often something on a foothold – a slight divot, a pebble, a ripple, a few fortuitously placed crystals – to aim for. *Appliance Friction* is one of the few where the rock is uniform enough in texture, and critically at just the right angle, to offer as close to a pure smearing test piece as you'll find at this grade. The finest of southern Peak gritstone means you'll want to keep your heels low, keep belief high and maintain focus all the way to the top to avoid an undignified slither back on to your pad.

The technical and sometimes bold arêtes, slabs and bulges in these woods have a history of being frequently rediscovered over the years since the 1970s, with intervening fallow periods in between as the undocumented problems are forgotten and the lichen and greenery returns. Since the publication of the BMC's *Froggatt to Black Rocks* guidebook in 2010, it seems that the main problems now see enough traffic to stay clean year-round. Sadly, the tall, overlapped slab of *Just Looking*, up and behind the boulder of *Appliance Friction*, is one which is reclaimed by the moss and pine needles more quickly than most – it offers another superb friction problem, but with a more committing feel, like a big gritstone smearing expedition. Worth seeking out when clean, but there's plenty of quality options here to fall back on if not.

Gwyneth Uttley keeps the faith in friction right to the very top.

DOLL TOR

8a Brainstorm

Although more well known for its Bronze Age stone circle, Doll Tor's rounded green blocks offer one or two worthwhile problems. Unlike much of the rock in the Stanton area their obscurity has saved them from the unwanted attention of vandals, leaving only beautifully weathered rounded Cratcliffe grit to search out.

Brainstorm started life as one of many variations on this lovely arête, all under the guise of *Gathering Storm*. Varying grades were offered depending on if a French start was used, or if it was started with a pull on from the block, or from the ground. Good value for anyone wanting to get three ticks without having to move their pads, but a little unsatisfactory for the purist. Ned Feehally's solution to the full low start, from the low break underneath the arête, is the logical culmination of these attempts to create a definitive problem on this arête – and it's such a sweet piece of rock it really deserves it. For the low start expect some full-bodied heelhooking, slapping and even knee-scums to turn the lip and get established on the upper section, where a couple of sloper moves and some tidy footwork should see you at the good little pocket way back over the top lip. Naturally, you've brushed the top-out before setting off, right?

The Andle Stone, which is passed on the walk-in, is increasingly shrouded by encroaching bushes, but just to the left of the ancient iron rungs and chipped holds there is a superb wall at 7b. It's worth the trip just to sample the various crimps, thumb sprags and other shenanigans leading to a final lunge for the top – brilliant.

A cocktail of power and subtlety hidden in the trees; Ned Feehally on the upper arête.

HILLCAR WOOD

 Dad's Arête (A Belly Full of Brad Berries)

Above the author on this infuriating micro-problem.
Opposite Ned Feehally on *Bigger than a Bee*.

A premium slice of Peak District esoterica, this frustrating arête lies tucked away in a secluded spot below a fairly inauspicious-looking quarry on the north-eastern edge of Stanton Moor. The quarry was once the site of a long-running protest camp, and *Dad's Arête* seems to protest vigorously against any attempts to climb it.

It has been suggested that the tree behind the block is gradually pushing and pushing, making the problem steeper and steeper every day as the tree grows. This is an intriguing idea; maybe this will be grit's first Font 9a eventually? The story goes a little way towards making those of us who've been completely shut down on the problem feel a little better about ourselves. However, the truth is we're probably just not good enough. A helpful-looking crimp near the top of the right-hand wall gives some hope, but the boulder's compact size and perfect landing belies the complexity of the task at hand. Good conditions, perseverance and impeccable technique will all be required to make any progress. Despite this, the arête's purity of form is hard to resist.

Luckily for those seeking a consolation prize, the crag does offer one or two more amenable challenges well worth seeking out. Most notable is *Bigger than a Bee*, a quality 7a on classic Cratcliffe-style rock, slopey handfuls of grit and clean smears – what's not to like?

TURNING STONE EDGE

 ## Salle Goose

Above cold weather mandatory; even then expect to try hard on *Salle Goose*. John Coefield climbing. © **Adam Long**
Opposite the author on the nearby *Birdsong*, one of the many recent additions to the Amber Valley. © **John Coefield**

Roche aux Sabots comes to the Amber Valley. Well, almost. In all fairness, the similarities to *Sale Gosse* in Fontainebleau don't extend further than the basic topography and style of the problem, so you will be spared the indignity of witnessing a sexagenarian Bleausard carrying nothing more than a pof rag and a hessian doormat casually waltz up this problem in the middle of your siege session. Small mercies.

Where Turning Stone can't compete with Sabots on the number of problems or proximity to patisseries, it's still a unique place to climb. Like the Chew Valley over to the west, the Ambler Valley has its own personality. With slightly different rock to the nearby Cratcliffe and Stanton crags, generally being finer grained and more angular in form, it sports some east-facing crag bands which are relatively rare on Peak grit. From your pads perched on the lofty rhododendron nest under *Salle Goose*, high above the trad routes, you can survey the valley sheltered from the prevailing westerlies. Although ironically you may actually want a little of the breeze to make the slopers on this problem feel a little better. Be warned, this Jon Fullwood problem is no pushover, and the long move to the top is a bit of a killer. Hard for the short, hard for the average height, and hard for the tall.

If you want to be transported from Roche aux Sabots to Chironico faster than a YouTuber in a campervan, then tumble down the gully just behind *Salle Goose* with your pads to find *River of Life* at the same grade but a complete contrast in style. One of the finest roof problems on grit, despite being a drop-off line. Definitely closer in style to problems in Ticino than the Forest, it benefits from a dry spell to ensure the starting holds aren't seeping. Not to mention some shoes with rubber over the toes – don't skip the crunches!

BLACK ROCKS

7a+ Velvet Silence

Homo sapiens seem to like order. It helps us understand stuff. We like to categorise things. We label plants and animals, the seasons, the weather, ourselves, our jobs, our hobbies. We compose photographs to make sense of the infinitely chaotic visual world around us, and likewise we arrange random sounds into something we understand to be music. We even break down the movement of climbing into a 'sequence'. But some things defy classification.

Velvet Silence at Black Rocks is both a route, and a boulder problem, and simultaneously neither. It has moves, but there is no sequence. It will not be clumsily codified as L-R-L-R-L-R. There is no 'top hold', the climb simply recedes off to the horizon over a distance of what feels like an eternity, yet it does definitely end. The green rock is neither clean nor dirty. It is neither natural nor chipped. Perfect yet flawed. The carved runnel is an aesthetically jarring scar tarnishing the perfection of a pristine slab. Yet, without it, the delicate friction moves to gain and then climb the beautiful rounded arête would not be attainable. Depending on who's eyes you look through it is simultaneously scary and steady, safe yet risky. It repels and attracts. It is inherently contradictory and hard to comprehend, yet in that moment of commitment it makes perfect sense.

So, what even is it – is it anything more than just a big chunk of rock? Perhaps that is enough.

Leave the down-turned shoes at home for this one. Clockwise from top, Pete Robins, Nige Kershaw, and Katy Whittaker. (Above and opposite © **John Coefield**; centre top and centre bottom © **Adam Long**.)

GRIT BLOCS

MAP

Problem	Grade	Page
1 Blood Sport	8a+	2
2 Jumping Jack Flash	6a+	4
3 George's Roof	7b+	6
4 Aurora	7a	10
5 Steve's Wall	5	12
6 Lay-by Arête	7b+	14
7 Cypher	8b	16
8 The Lash	7c+	18
9 Phoenix Wall	7b+	20
10 Successor State	7a	22
11 Fluide	7c	24
12 Trust	7a+	26
13 Snaketongue Truffleclub	6c	28
14 Heaven in Your Hands	7c	30
15 Damnation	8a	32
16 Rhythm	8a+	34
17 Molly Moocher	7a+	36
18 Lanny Bassham	8b	38
19 Poetry in Motion	6b	40
20 Greg's Arête Right	4+	42
21 Jason's Roof	7c+	44
22 Ron's Crack II	7a+	46
23 Ill Gotten Gains	7c+	48
24 Victoria's Secret	7b+	50
25 McNab	7b	52
26 Bird Flu	7a+	54
27 Hunter's Roof	7c	56
28 Flying Arête	6b	58
29 Syrett's Roof	6c+	60
30 Ben's Groove	7b	62
31 High Fidelity	8b	64
32 The Geminid Trail	7a+	66
33 Brownian Motion	8a+	68
34 Frank	7c+	70
35 Lager Lager Lager (Dave's Groove)	7c	72
36 The John Dunne Slap	6b	74
37 Treebeard	7c	76
38 Vim	6a+	78
39 Red Baron Roof	7c+	80
40 Gritty Shaker	7c	82
41 Androsterone	7a	84
42 Fight on Black	7b	86
43 Chabal	8a	88
44 Needle of Dreams	6c	90
45 Tony's Wall	7b+	92
46 Red Rooster	7c	94
47 Ouzel Thorn	6b	98
48 Bad Moon Rising	7b+	100
49 Mothership Reconnection	7a+	102
50 The Square	6a	104

Problem	Grade	Page
51 Archery	7a	108
52 Fish Arête Sit-Start	7b	110
53 Cazu Marzu	7c	112
54 Unnamed arête	7-ish	114
55 Panopticon	7c+	116
56 Perfect Porthole Problem	5+	118
57 Master Kush	7c+	120
58 Spike	7b	122
59 Solomon Grundy	8a	124
60 D.I.Y.	6b	126
61 Careless Torque	8a	128
62 The High Road	3+	130
63 West Side Story	7b+	132
64 All Quiet on the Eastern Front	6a+	134
65 Cleo's Edge	5+	136
66 Boyager	7a+	138
67 The Alliance	7a+	140
68 Sidepull Arch	5+	142
69 The Big Slab	4+	144
70 Technical Master	6b	146
71 Pet Cemetery	7a+	148
72 Les Grand Doigts	7c	150
73 Ill Behaviour	8a+	152
74 Hot Toddy	7a+	154
75 The Art of White Hat Wearing	7b	156
76 Smiling Buttress	8-ish	158
77 Curbar Corner	5+	160
78 A Beagle Too Far	6b	162
79 I Like Ya Cut G	7c	164
80 G-Thang	6b+	166
81 Superbloc	8a+	168
82 HMS Daring	7b+	170
83 Darkthrone	7b	172
84 Proper Gander	7c	174
85 Hard Arête	7a+	176
86 Finger of Fate	6b	178
87 Swivel Finger	6b	180
88 Original Starlight and Storm	6c+	182
89 Charlie's Overhang	6b	184
90 Elephant's Ear	4+	186
91 Tierdrop	7a+	188
92 Big Al Qaeda	7b	190
93 Egg Arête	6a+	192
94 Brain Dead	6c	194
95 Spare Rib (Brutal Arête)	7b	196
96 Appliance Friction	6b	198
97 Brainstorm	8a	200
98 Dad's Arête (A Belly Full of Brad Berries)	7c	202
99 Salle Goose	7c+	204
100 Velvet Silence	7a+	206

209

EPILOGUE

Having reached the end of our journey through the many shapes, colours and flavours of gritstone bouldering, we should review why we set out on this in the first place.

Firstly, thinking back to *Bleau Blocs*, we wanted to see if what we have matches up well against Fontainebleau. Can we look the Bleausards squarely in the eye and say the cream of Pennine grit is up there with the best of the best? I would like to think that we can. The abundance of top quality per square mile in Font perhaps can't be matched, but as far as sheer quality goes we're golden.

Secondly, we set out to celebrate the whole spectrum of the best gritstone bouldering. Have we achieved this? Well, we've covered the full geographic spread of the Pennine gritstone areas, we've passed through nine counties, from high moorland to post-industrial quarries, shady woodland to winter suntraps, quiet undocumented tors to popular roadside crags. World-famous problems to unheard-of hidden gems. We've looked at all levels of difficulty, from problems close to beginner standard right up to unrepeated state-of-the-art lines. The old and the new. But have we really captured a full picture of the best of grit bouldering? With no fixed definition of what the best actually is, can we ever really know?

I can assure you that embarking on a project like this is a daunting task. Matters concerning what is the best, what quality means and what is of value are highly subjective. As a species, human beings are not capable of reaching a consensus on matters as simple as whether you put clotted cream on a scone first or jam, so picking the top 100 grit problems is a tough ask. And with literally thousands of problems to choose from on gritstone, the statistical odds of anyone's favourite individual problem being included in the book are slim. The chances of any two people being in complete agreement with this list of 100 problems? Close to zero. So, I'm on to a loser here before I've even started. I can't please everyone, or indeed anyone. But with this realisation comes a huge sense of release, because there's no point even trying to please everyone. Definitive? We can't do definitive. Authoritative? Now maybe that's achievable.

The truth is, with the richness of gritstone, the depth of quality we have, you could easily produce this book five times over with a different set of problems each time and still have a fairly complete picture of the best of the best in any given book. We should celebrate this embarrassment of riches and roll with it.

Your 100 favourites will be different to mine. In fact, I would encourage everyone to go out and find their own. Don't take my word for it, and certainly don't just plough through this book like a ticklist. If you've bought the book to try and tick everything you should take it out and burn it. Well, don't burn it as that would release sequestered carbon into the atmosphere. Instead, dispose of it in a responsible manner. Perhaps donate it to someone less fortunate – a charity shop, or your mate who only climbs on limestone. And then go and buy another copy because you want inspiration to experience the entire gamut of what gritstone can mean.

Go out and find those experiences. Go and check some new places out. Don't just go to Stanage and Burbage, Caley and Almscliff. Don't just climb the things you see in videos; don't just do the low-hanging fruit. Don't even limit yourselves to things which have already been climbed. Get out there and put the legwork in; follow your nose. Experience the highs and the lows, the epic days, the disappointments, the split tips, the amazing crisp clear winter sessions under cobalt blue skies, the damp washouts, the spectacular sunsets. Do problems that suit you, and do ones you're terrible at. Waltz up something you've previously written off, and inexplicably fail on something despite having trained hard. Suffer a bit. Then find those sublime moments where everything clicks, and you float up a problem almost without trying. Find those problems where the concentration flips into a sort of meditative state. It's this range of possible experiences that gritstone excels at, that other rock types struggle to match. That's what makes it special; that's why the best days on grit are the best days climbing you will ever have. See you out there.

GRADES

The thorny topic of grades, a subject we British seem to be obsessed with. We may as well be on an understanding about this – grades are a nonsense at the best of times. In the same way that we can't achieve any sort of meaningful consensus on what quality means, we also can't expect too much from the grading system. On the surface it is doomed to fail; we are trying to measure difficulty (which isn't measurable), we are trying to bench-mark it against some sort of fixed standard (and that standard doesn't and can't exist) and expecting it to be a useful piece of information for climbers of all ages, shapes and sizes and in all conditions (fundamentally impossible) and be consistent globally (again …).

Given the above, it's a minor miracle that any climbing grading system works at all. And having ridiculed the entire endeavour, I will counter with the suggestion that many of the shortcomings of any grading system can be sidestepped by simply remembering what we are grading, and what it's for. We're grading problems – the passages up or along the rock – and we're doing it so a piece of information exists for someone who's never been to the crag or doesn't know the problem. Once you've been there and you're in some way familiar with the problem then the grade's job is done and you can forget about it.

Put more simply; we don't grade ascents. 'I'm taking 7c for that' – are you? Where are you taking it? It's still here, because the grade is attached to the problem. The grade is not a measure of performance. It's not a medal or an achievement, and it can change as soon as a better sequence is found, a hold breaks, or at the whim of the next guidebook writer. If you run five kilometres but it feels really hard one day for some reason you don't get to say you've run six kilometres do you? If that five kilometres felt easy you don't conclude maybe it was only four kilometres. If we abandon all this 'taking the grade' business then things start to make a lot more sense again.

So don't get too hung up about grades. They are presented in this book broadly as stated in the most recent guides, unless the weight of the prevailing consensus has somehow made itself felt by the author one way or another. It's nothing personal, I promise.

Madeleine Cope on *Crescent Arête*, Stanage.

ACKNOWLEDGEMENTS

I'm indebted to quite a few people for their support with this book, one way or another. First and foremost, my immediate family, and especially my amazing wife Helen, supporting me through thick and thin and generally putting up with my jokes and tolerating me being a pain in the arse all the time when I'm not climbing or taking photos. My sister Heather, who thankfully is a much better writer than I am, gave me numerous pointers on the writing process and is a legend in her own right. Also, thanks go to all the crew at Vertebrate Publishing for all their hard work on this book, and not least John Coefield for having the confidence in me to set the whole ball rolling with this book. If you don't like the book, then basically blame John cos it's his fault.

When undertaking a project like this local knowledge is key. This is especially important now more than ever. Crucially, it makes the difference between the increasingly algorithm-controlled data-driven portrayal of climbing we see online, and what is genuinely a careful, curated piece of work coming from a position of a genuine love for climbing and gritstone in particular. With that in mind I would like to thank the following local experts and activists who contributed in some way towards formulating and finalising the list of problems for this book, for fielding questions, bouncing opinions around, putting me in touch with other climbers to photograph, and generally being supportive of the entire endeavour. Legends all: Paul Bennett, Rachel Briggs, Tom Briggs, Will Buck, John Coefield, Tom Crane, Steve Dunning, Andy Emery, Ned Feehally, Jon Fullwood, Adam Long, David Mason, Robin Mueller, Jason Pickles, Mark Sharratt, Rob Smith, Matt Thompson and Andi Turner.

A special thanks goes to Andy Emery for generously dispensing his considerable knowledge pertaining to all matters geological. Without Andy's input I would still think gritstone came out of volcanoes and Carboniferous means you only eat really burnt food. It turns out it's all just river sludge. Who knew?

In addition to the above, a huge thanks goes to all those climbers and spotters who were willing to endure the intrusion of having a camera pointed at them while climbing. This includes people I bumped into at the crag randomly over the years, friends and acquaintances, and more recently to those who I'd only just met yet were generous enough with their time to head out to all corners of the Pennines to climb problems specifically for this book. The book could not have happened without you all: Naomi Abboud, Emma Banks, Frances Bensley, Delon Blair, Ben Bransby, Tom Briggs, Adam Coefeld, John Coefield, Lawrence Cooper, Ross Cooper, Madeleine Cope, Tom Crane, Pete Dawson, Jinalee De Silva, Andy Emery, Laurence Everitt, Ned Feehally, Jon Fullwood, Marco Giudice, Louise Hall, Andy Harris, Henry Jeffreys, Tyler Landman, Mina Leslie-Wujastyk, Kim Leyland, Adam Long, Julia Mariella, David Mason, Martin Mobråten, Ben Morton, Dave Norton, George Norton, James Parrott, William Parry, Tom Peckitt, Jason Pickles, Jim Pope, Steve Royle, Laurie Smith, Martin Smith, Rob Smith, Matt Thompson, Gwyneth Uttley, Char Williams, Simon Wilson and Toby Wilson.

I've been lucky enough to be able to lean on a number of skilled and experienced photographers who have provided images for the book. In addition to logistical pragmatism, their involvement adds an extra dimension to the book. Every photographer's vision is different; everyone reads the shapes of the rock, the quality of light, and the interaction with the climber in their own way. Everyone brings a little something different to the table, but all united by a fondness for the grit. Hopefully this affection shines through. Thanks to Nick Brown, Michele Caminati, John Coefield, Mike Delderfield, Sam Lawson, Adam Long, Oliver Parkinson, Sam Pratt, Elis Rees, Mark Sharratt, Rowan Spear-Bulmer, Darren Stevenson, Dave Sutcliffe, Owen Tomkins, James Turnbull and Ray Wood.

Finally, thanks to the late MF DOOM for providing the soundtrack to keep me sane during innumerable long drives up and down the M1 and around the B-roads of Yorkshire over the last few months of this project.